To Michelle
Thank you so much for your support in our fight for LARCP & vet

Barbara

Barbara B. Wilson LCSW,

THE
MENTAL
HEALTH
HANDBOOK

A Guide to Understanding California's Mental Health System

Barbara B. Wilson, MSW, LCSW, EDPNA

ACKNOWLEDGEMENTS

This manual was created during the COVID-19 quarantine. No one creates a project alone. I am no exception. For the first time in more than a decade, I was forced to be indoors for a long period of time. I did not make house calls or engage in providing face-to-face services or in-person advocacy. I have "a pandemic" to thank for giving me the time needed to focus on creating this handbook.

I thank Sylvia Edwards and Suzanne Lishon for combing through my writing line by line and asking me hard questions about the words I was choosing. These wonderful wordsmiths gave of themselves, their time, and their skills to edit this manuscript. Where would I have been without "boy wonder", Justin Torres? He does magical things with computers, things I will never understand. Silvia Chitgian, a newly minted social worker, gave of her time both in editing this handbook and in giving service to mothers who have adult children with Serious Mental Illness. I must also thank the many friends and clients who have nudged me along, saying, "Barbara, you need to write all that stuff down in a book."

Many thanks to those of you who read the manuscript and gave me feedback. While some of you wish to remain anonymous, I want to acknowledge your willingness to give thoughtful comments.

To my family, Nicole and Tony Wilson, thank you for your continued support throughout these years. Nicole, you are not only a wonderful, thoughtful and caring daughter but you have grown up to become an astute administrator. Your parents have learned so much from you as you translate technology for us. Many thanks for sharing your time and expertise to help with this project.

This book is dedicated to all the children, young adults, and older adults who have ever had a thought disorder and to their families who learned that love was not enough.

This handbook provides the following:

- A brief overview of the history of mental health policy, both at the federal level and within the State of California.

- A description of the trauma often experienced by the parents of an adult with serious and persistent forms of mental illness.

- Recommendations of minimal basic elements that any public mental health care system should include.

- Basic material helpful to families with family members who have serious mental illness.

- A description of the Mental Health Hookup model for addressing personal and family challenges in coping with serious mental illness.

Author's note: All images embedded in document are public facing or purchased from ShutterStock ™

Who is this information for?

PEOPLE	
Parents, Grandparents	Siblings
Bus Drivers	Teachers and Educational Administrators
Care Givers	Retail and Public Facing employees
Chaplains/ Religious Practitioners	Property Managers
Elected Officials/ Policy Makers	Mental Health Clinicians
Emergency Medical Technicians	First Responders
Public Facing Civil Servants	

ORGANIZATIONS	
After school programs	Chamber of Commerce
Behavioral Health Centers	Public Facing Entities
Youth Organizations	Parks and Recreation
Corporate Foundations	School Districts
Homeowner Associations	Small Local Business Associations
Hospitals	Tourism Boards
Law Enforcement	Trade Organizations
Libraries	Civic Organizations
Retail Establishments	

Why would this information be helpful to such a wide sector of communities?

Because it would help to inform their staff members on how to engage with adults who are experiencing symptoms of serious mental illness.

Table of Contents

CHAPTER 1
MENTAL HEALTH IN THE UNITED STATES

Mental Health Policy in the 19th and 20th Centuries

The birth of separate and protective housing for adults with symptoms of serious mental illness (SMI) came from the advocacy of Dorothea Dix. Dorothea Dix was the oldest child of a pastor who traveled and drank alcohol to excess and a mother who was prone to "bouts of depression." At age 12, she moved to Boston, where she lived with a wealthy aunt. By age 14, she was teaching poor girls to read.

Dorothea Dix (1802-1887)
Mother of Mental Health Policy in America
Social Reformer

Dorothea Dix later visited both public and private prisons, documenting the horrors she discovered, including but not limited to brutal physical and sexual abuse—both by other inmates and by staff members—filth, withholding food and clothing, and keeping inmates chained. She presented her findings to the Massachusetts legislature. She advocated for the creation of a different option that provided for the protection of these patients and improvement in their care. Stunned by her reports, the Massachusetts legislature established funds to create the first "mental hospital" in Worcester.

Dorothea Dix continued her advocacy and helped create similar state-funded institutions in other locations such as Rhode Island, New York, and parts of Europe. Following service as an administrator and advocate for nurses in the American Civil War, Dorothea Dix resumed her advocacy on behalf of adults with mental illness for the remainder of her life. She died at age 85.

The growth of state-funded hospitals for adults with psychosis became the model of treatment nationwide throughout much of the 20th century. Often state hospitals were located in remote areas far from population centers.

Seeking "the Cure" for Serious Mental Illness

Social Darwinism, a theory that postulated "survival of the fittest," was a popular concept of the late 19th century. If all the "mental defectives" were kept from reproducing, the argument went, mental health problems would disappear.

Historical marker of Indiana Eugenics Law.

Indiana was the first of more than 30 states to enact a compulsory sterilization law allowing the state to "prevent procreation of confirmed criminals, idiots, imbeciles and rapists." ("Social Darwinism." Encyclopedia Britannica)

1907: Indiana Begins a New Cure for Serious Mental Illness—Sterilization

Influencer Harry H. Laughlin, the Director of Eugenics in Cold Spring Harbor, New York, published a book in 1922 titled *Eugenical Sterilization in the United States*. In Chapter XV he presented a "Model Eugenical Sterilization Law," which formed the basis of the Virginia Sterilization Act of 1924. In a legal case, *Buck* v. *Bell*, the United States Supreme Court upheld the constitutionality of this act. By 1924, at least 15 states had passed similar laws, and 24 states had done likewise by 1956.

Central State Hospital (Virginia)

Sterilization was routinely performed on both males and females diagnosed with mental illness or other neurological issues such as seizures or intellectual disabilities. At its core, this policy of sterilization had tremendous public support since it was seen as a way to reduce costs to taxpayers associated with providing care for "mental defectives." By 1940, 18,552 people with mental illness had been surgically sterilized.

After 1988, the Virginia law was amended to require "informed consent." A physician was required to inform the patient prior to sterilization that it was going to happen.

A court order to authorize sterilization was based on criteria such as:

- Likely to engage in sexual activities.

- Permanence of mental disability.

- Projected inability to be a proper parent.

- Lack of access to other forms of contraception.

The court order authorized sterilization on a *mentally incompetent* adult or child. The procedure conformed with medical standards and medical sterilization. It became a prevalent practice.

In 2001–2002 the Virginia legislature passed a joint resolution apologizing for the Commonwealth's past participation in eugenics and established a path for reparations.

The Next Big Cures for Serious Mental Illness: Early 20th Century Psychiatric Practices

Before the discovery of psychotropic medication, mental health care providers used specific techniques to treat patients experiencing delusions, hearing voices, seeing things others couldn't see, and smelling things others couldn't smell. Doctors in the United States and abroad sought treatment techniques that would quiet the tortuous symptoms and hallmarks of severe mental illness.

- **Hydrotherapy:** Hydrotherapy was a common psychiatric practice used to treat mental illness with alternating extended baths with temperatures varying from cold to warm depending on the symptoms.

- **Insulin Shock Therapy:** Insulin shock therapy involved administering insulin in order to induce an insulin coma meant to produce a reduction in symptoms associated with psychosis. Later the coma would be ended by injecting an IV solution of glucose or warm saline solution

- **Metrazol:** Metrazol was a stimulant often used to induce seizures, but it presented significant problems with side effects.

- **Electroshock Therapy/Electroconvulsive Therapy (ECT):** Electroshock therapy represented a new technique to induce small seizures in a controlled setting. Psychiatrists observed that many patients with seizure disorders seemed to have improved moods following such events. Logic dictated that if seizures could be artificially created, this could/would improve mental disorders.

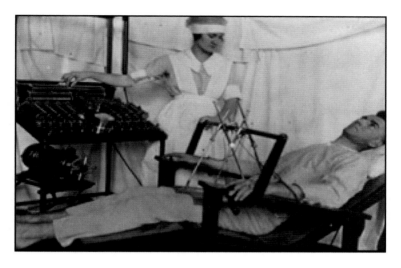

1938 - Italian neurologist Ugo Cerlitti introduces electroshock therapy as a treatment for people with schizophrenia and other chronic mental illnesses.

Despite the fact that these techniques were common in the early 20th century, many states continued to use hydrotherapy, insulin therapy, and ECT until the mid-20th century, when chemical medications began to be used.

Brain Surgery as the Cure for Serious Mental Illness

In 1936, Dr. James Watt and his colleague Dr. Walter Freeman performed the first brain surgery in the United States, the lobotomy, which sought to cure SMI. Dr. Egas Moniz had already performed this technique in Portugal in 1935. The original collaborators, Drs. Watt and Freeman, parted company over the issue of which technique was superior: transorbital or surgical.

The surgical method, as performed by Dr. Moniz, "required drilling holes in the patient's skull to get to the brain." Dr. Watt continued to perform lobotomies using this method. The transorbital method, developed by Dr. Freeman, required no drilling. Patients were administered electroshock in order to induce unconsciousness followed by the insertion of an ice pick–like instrument entering through each eye to access the frontal lobes. We are fortunate to have a person with lived experience describe his experience of having a lobotomy performed upon him as a 12-year old boy. (See Howard Dully's Testimony.

Dr. Watt and Dr. Freeman

The novel, *One Flew Over the Cuckoo's Nest*, by Ken Kesey, used the fear of a forced lobotomy as a central issue for the main character. It was later made into a movie. By the late 1950s an estimated 50,000 lobotomies had been performed in the United States. Ultimately, the lobotomy fell out of favor while Freudian psychotherapy techniques and the introduction of pharmacological products gained more popularity as a way to control symptoms.

Recognizing the Need for Research: We Don't Know How to Cure Serious Mental Illness

President Harry Truman establishes the National Mental Health Act

In 1946, President Harry Truman signed the National Mental Health Act. The act called for the establishment of the National

Institute of Mental Health (NIMH) and acknowledged the need for national funding to promote research, especially in the realm of serious and persistent mental illness.

Beliefs about the causes of SMI varied and often focused on blame. Scapegoats included:

- Genes.

- Family upbringing.

- Evil demons or spirits.

The Promise of Medications

The community mental health movement was created as a way for people with SMI to live in society. It evolved with the use of pharmaceuticals. Mental health care professionals began to use pharmaceuticals to control symptoms of SMI such as hallucinations, delusions, depression, and mania. The drugs seemed to promise a permanent solution for the management of mental illness in US society. The possibilities of pharmaceuticals seemed endless; and, it seemed as though people with SMI could be reintegrated into American society with minimal expense to taxpayers. Additionally, a change in Medicaid regulations spurred the depopulation of the nation's mental hospitals.

President John F. Kennedy

During his administration President John Kennedy signed legislation to move mental health care away from the state hospital model and into the community. Although his vision was derailed because of the necessity of funding for the Vietnam War, a national movement continued to evolve during the Johnson era to bring mental health treatment into community settings as part of the War on Poverty.

Timeline of Mental Health Legislation

- **1963**: President John F. Kennedy signed the Community Mental Health Act to provide federal funding for research and the construction of community-based treatment facilities.

- **1980:** President Jimmy Carter signed the Mental Health Systems Act, which established a nationwide plan to phase out state hospitals and build smaller mental health centers closer to communities. This bill was passed in 1980 but was never implemented due to its repeal the following year.

President Jimmy Carter

- **1981:** Newly elected President Ronald Reagan successfully repealed the Mental Health Systems Act via the Omnibus Budget Reconciliation Act, which established block grants for the states, ending the federal government's role in providing services to adults with SMI. "Block grants" established the principle that the federal government transferred tax monies to each state for its use. Each state then established its priorities for the distribution of those funds. As a result, mental health care was almost never funded.

President Ronald Reagan

- **1984**: Federal mental-health spending decreases by 30 percent by 1984 and reflects an uptick in homelessness among people suffering from SMI

The Ohio-based study, (Roth, Bean, Stefl, and Howe, Homelessness in Ohio) finds that up to 30 percent of homeless people are thought to suffer from serious mental illness. (NIH)

Police outreach to homeless person

Current Status

By 2021 in the United States, we had come full circle. We were providing housing for adults with SMI in jails and prisons. Aside from the inhumanity of this solution, it was also expensive and ineffective.

Case Study #1: By 2015, the largest mental health treatment facility in Los Angeles County for acute mental illness was the Los Angeles County Jail. The Los Angeles County Board of Supervisors ordered an assessment of the effectiveness of incarcerating adults with SMI. (https://da.lacounty.gov/sites/default/files/policies/Mental-Health-Report-072915.pdf)

Findings: The belief was that all people can learn a connection between behavior and negative consequences (incarceration). The research showed, however, that many persons who have SMI fail to connect their behavior with incarceration so that they repeat those same behaviors.

Costs: Because adults with SMI are often low-income individuals, once arrested and incarcerated, they utilize a high level of publicly funded resources such as court time, public defenders, district attorneys, housing in jails, and transportation costs, with additional costs that may include the use of a psychiatric emergency team and overuse of the emergency room. The study found that incarcerating people with mental illness costs more taxpayer money than providing excellent mental health treatment. By default, the single largest mental health treatment provider in Los Angeles, California, is its jail.

Ethics: Incarcerating offenders with a psychiatric (medical) disorder leads us to ask: is it ethical to incarcerate people who commit a crime as the result of a mental disorder versus providing treatment for the disorder?

Recommendations:

- Establish and/or increase mental health care access and treatment, especially for low-level nonviolent, nonsexual crimes.

- Provide basic mental health care training to law enforcement officers.

- Add mental health personnel to accompany law enforcement officers on calls.

- Create mental health liaisons to be co-located in county courtrooms to facilitate early recognition of persons appearing in court who are in need of mental health screenings and services.

Case Study #2: A 2020 RAND Study in Los Angeles, California looked at the feasibility of diverting more inmates to community-based mental health housing and treatment versus incarceration. Here are some of the results:

- In a single month (June 2019) 5,544 out of 17,204 inmates were in mental health housing units and/or on psychotropic medication.

- Some 61% of those inmates with mental illness (about 3,368 people) could be appropriately diverted into community-based services or support-ive housing.

- Women were more likely to be eligible for diversion than men, even though the majority of adults with SMI were male.

- Housing and the provision of community-based mental health services provided significant savings to taxpayers.

Where are the beds?

Unfortunately, implementation of these studies are hampered because of the decreasing supply of community beds.

Summary

Awareness of the need to provide specialized services to adults with SMI began in the 1800s with one crusader, Dorothea Dix. Since then, Americans have sought various solutions both to provide cures and/or management of symptoms and to contain costs of treatment. From prisons, to state hospitals, to the abdication of treatment, back to prisons, we as a nation have gone full circle. Yet we stand at a time of great opportunity for the creation of a new system of care that integrates both public and private resources—one that is humane and provides for the dignity and self-worth of every single person, one that is cost-effective yet of high quality, one that provides protective services for both the person with mental illness and for the family, one that provides protection for society. Impossible? Not at all.

CHAPTER 2
PHILOSOPHY OF PUBLIC MENTAL HEALTH TREATMENT

As history shows, America has vacillated in its treatment of people who have SMI. On one hand, we have seen treatment with compassion and potential rehabilitation. On the other hand, we have seen punitive measures and the withholding of treatment often based on the promise of saving taxpayers' money. In this chapter, we follow the ebb and flow between providing treatment and withholding treatment as our national (i.e., federal) policy.

There are many examples of policy changes based on this dichotomy of philosophies. The policy to sterilize adults with SMI against their will derived much of its popularity with taxpayers from the belief that it would save public taxpayer money. In much the same way, the rapid depopulation of state mental hospitals was based on a policy change and the desire to save money.

In 1965, Congress created Medicaid and Medicare. People with mental illness were specifically excluded from eligibility for benefits if they were in a state hospital. The result, intentionally or unintentionally, motivated states to shift the cost of care for adults with SMI to the federal government. This could be achieved by moving "patients" from the state hospitals to the community where they could then become eligible for federally funded Medicaid (MediCal in California).(Placzek, KQED.org.)

The policy of creating rehabilitation for adults with SMI first appeared under the Kennedy administration. Fortunately, despite Kennedy's assassination, his policies continued to transform mental health care from an institution-based to a community-based system. The view that the federal government should provide funding for a basic level of mental health care stemmed from the Kennedy presidency. President Kennedy advocated for the creation of what became known as the Community Mental Health Act. Its purpose was to promote a nationwide system of community-based care for people with SMI and for people with intellectual disabilities. At that time, conditions in state mental hospitals varied considerably across the nation. Few national standards of care existed. Private health organizations and health insurers often specifically excluded mental illness from coverage. It is now known that the president had a sister who had received a failed lobotomy—he had a family member with mental illness.

Despite the fact that the Community Mental Health Act was never fully funded due to the increased monies diverted to those fighting the growing Vietnam conflict, there was significant activism and emphasis on a new field: community psychiatry. Various formats of community programs emerged as state systems struggled with issues of liability and co-locating with other community organizations such as churches, community centers, and library community rooms. Lawsuits were filed as mental health care practitioners joined coalitions to advocate for legal reforms empowering adults with SMI. Additionally, there was hope and enthusiasm within the mental health care community due to the promise of the use of psychotropic medications.

The Birth of Supplemental Security Income

During this period of deinstitutionalization of state hospitals, (1975) Supplemental Security Income (SSI) was created. Supplemental Security Income resulted at least partially from a federal government survey examining how funding for "Aid to the Totally Blind and Disabled" was being implemented across the country. The survey revealed:

- Huge disparities in how the funding was spent.

- Lack of national uniform minimum standards.

- Fraud.

- Racial bias toward black citizens. (e.g., Local welfare departments frequently failed to inform potentially eligible applicants that such programs were available.)

The federal government took action and created SSI. It established a uniform base of federal eligibility and a uniform federal payment structure. Effective January 1, 1974, the Social

Security Administration was tasked to administer the application and payment.

One unintended consequence of the creation of the SSI program was the transfer of the cost of treatment of people with SMI to the federal government and away from the states (state hospitals). For example, the cost of hospitalization per person was $13,835 annually at a New York state psychiatric hospital. By simply transferring that person to a boarding house, the cost would be $4,600 because SSI would pay the living costs, thereby saving the state more than $9,000 per year. (Torrey, E. F. p 87).

In 1980, President Jimmy Carter continued the march toward federal funding for the construction of community mental health centers, a sure sign that only the most seriously ill people would be hospitalized involuntarily. A year later, this most important puzzle piece that provided for successful transfer from remotely located state hospital treatment to local community-based construction was repealed.

The Reagan Philosophy of Mental Health Treatment

Let's take a brief look at Governor Ronald Reagan's philosophy regarding public funding of care and treatment for adults with SMI: what did Reagan allegedly believe?

First, prevention cannot be proven. Even when a mental health care provider works with a person and that person makes a desirable change in his/her behavior, no one can prove 100% that the changed behavior was due to the interventions. No special training is required to work with adults with SMI. All that is required is common sense.

Second, taxpayer monies should not be spent on people with mental illness. Those expenses should be borne by a patient's family. Closing state hospitals would save the taxpayers money (failing to mention that there would be a rise in law-and-order costs since there were few community mental health programs to replace/reintegrate former state hospital "patients" back into the community).

California became a leader of the deinstitutionalization movement. An avid proponent of the transformation of the role of government, Reagan promoted the philosophy that government should not provide direct services. Rather, the government should perform only regulatory functions. Additionally, Governor Reagan had close political ties with for-profit chains that opened board-and-care homes, often clustered in low-income communities. A study completed as early as 1969 noted the "state-hospital-like atmosphere" in board-and-care homes. (Torrey, p.87)

By 1972, California saw an uptick of the incarceration of men with serious mental disorders. These results were documented in a paper written by Dr. Marc Abramson, titled "The Criminalization of Mentally Disordered Behavior." Despite these events on the ground, Governor Reagan sold California taxpayers on the savings they would gain as the direct result of the rapid closure of state hospitals. Like employees of many large organizations, mental health care workers, as employees, were discouraged from speaking truths. Both public and private organizations have paid information officers who speak for the organization. Government is no exception.

While it is challenging to locate specific works on Reagan as governor, there are a few that reflect his views. Sociologist Colin Samson wrote an article, "Inequality, the New Right and Mental Health Care Delivery in the United States in the Reagan Era". There is also a masters thesis of history by Ryan Catney entitled "A Laboratory of Social Policy: California, the New Right and the Gubernatorial Administration of Ronald Reagan, 1967-1975 (Queen's University, Kingston, Ontario)".

Eventually, Governor Reagan soared in a popular presidential election where he promptly overturned the 1980 Carter plan to create smaller, local community mental health care centers and close state hospitals on a gradual basis. By 1985 a report from Los Angeles estimated that 30-50% of homeless persons were adults with SMI, seen in "ever increasing numbers."(Torrey, p. 102) At the same time, adults with SMI and homeless persons were becoming an object of national concern. During the 1980s, the number of adults with SMI in jails and prisons was also increasing.

Reports of significant increases in jails and prisons housing people with SMI began to surface from rural and urban states across the country. Reports also began to cite an uptick in violent behaviors, some of which involved gun violence, which generated media coverage.

By the 1990's, the era of placing mostly institutionalized "former patients" into the community had devolved into an era of placing people who were often "hard to place" due to their hard-to-manage behaviors. This situation was combined with various court decisions, one of which was the inability to force medications. Additionally, reports emerged of an increase of violence toward staff and other residents. At this time, no additional federal funds were available for adults with SMI except SSI and Medicaid. This often resulted in annual budget cuts to the few mental health programs targeted to adults with SMI. Few, if any states, chose to spend their block grant funding on providing mental health services. By default, in cities like Chicago, New York, Los Angeles, and Miami, the largest acute psychiatric hospitals across the nation, became the county jails.

Frequently Asked Questions

Did the deinstitutionalization of psychiatric hospitals save taxpayers money?

No. A report submitted to the Los Angeles County Board of Supervisors in 2015 indicated that the cost of NOT treating an adult with SMI was actually greater than the cost of high-quality mental health treatment. (LA County, Mental Health Report)

A RAND study found that many incarcerated people with mental illness could be better served and at a lower cost to taxpayers if they were diverted into community programs. (Holliday, Stephanie Brooks, et al)

Is there a reason taxpayer money should be used to fund programs for adults with SMI?

Yes. The average age of onset of SMI is often young adult-hood, precisely when a young person is engaged in career build-ing. (NAMI.org) People between the ages of 16 and 29 are often attending college, serving in the military, or working some sort of entry-level job they hope will lead to a career. The onset of their mental illness disrupts that process. Subsequent episodes of psychosis serve to derail their self-image and goals as they struggle to understand what has happened to them. Even people who develop SMI after they've graduated college and embarked on a career path may lose any employment-related benefits, including Social Security Disability (SSD), depending on their journey of acceptance/denial of their mental disability. Dedicated public funding provides an essential bridge for adults with SMI. (www.NAMI.org)

Summary

It is difficult to comprehend that we can put a man on the moon, but we have not created a way to identify those at risk of developing SMI. Schizophrenia—called by other names in other cultures and periods of history—is one of the oldest diseases known to mankind. Serious mental illness does not respect race, class, or intelligence. We do know, however, that SMI will often lead to poverty in America.

The "toggle" between providing therapeutic care or saving taxpayer monies has proven to be a false choice. By abdicating any dedicated federal funding to provide services to people with SMI, we have actually spent more local and state taxpayer dollars since law enforcement systems are more costly than mental health treatment systems. Additionally, the outcomes have been abysmal and inhumane as we have treated our brethren as throwaways.

CHAPTER 3
THE FEDERAL SYSTEM

The Americans with Disabilities Act 1990

While much mental health policy is decided by specific legislation, significant changes can also come from court decisions. For example, the Americans with Disabilities Act was not originally intended to cover mental disabilities, but a court decision granted inclusion. When the Americans with Disabilities Act (ADA) was passed in 1990, little thought was given to whether disabilities **included** mental disabilities and/or intellectual disabilities. The intention of the legislation was to provide recognition of visible disabilities.

To address the lack of mention of mental disabilities, the US Supreme Court decision in *Olmstead* v. *L.C.*, 527 U.S. 581 (1999) decreed mental health patients had the right to be treated in the "least restrictive setting" possible rather than automatically placing a person in a hospital setting. While the case involved people with intellectual disabilities rather than psychiatric disabilities, its significance is that it established that persons with mental illness are disabled. They could reside in the community.

The *Olmstead* decision firmly placed mental illness in the disability category. This inclusion was to prove significant, particularly in employment and disability law.

The path for equitable recognition and, therefore, equitable treatment for the disabling symptoms of SMI was and remains an ongoing fight. Like so many battles for equality, however, these fights are essential and worthwhile if we are to apply our Constitution to everyone.

Health Insurance Portability and Accountability Act (HIPAA) 1996

The Health Insurance Portability and Accountability Act (HIPAA) is another example of federal legislation with honorable motives and massive unintended consequences for the mental health community. Previous to the passage of this legislation, patients' personal data such as their name, contact information, and medical diseases were being sold to for-profit organizations without their knowledge or consent. This law was passed to solve that problem.

One of the unintended consequences of HIPAA for people in the mental health community, especially family members, is the inability to coordinate care or even to locate their family members. Parents, in particular, often have their family members transported by ambulance or law enforcement officers *to where*? Hospital staff members are not permitted to acknowledge that they do or do not have *a particular person on their treatment unit* unless and until the person in question signs a Release of Information.

New Federal Dollars

The Mental Health Parity and Addiction Equity Act (2008)

Under the Mental Health Parity and Addiction Equity Act (2008) federal law declared it to be illegal for health insurers to surcharge or refuse coverage for mental health treatment. Previously, insurance companies had no standards requiring mental health care coverage. Coverage varied widely as to whether the insured was covered to see a mental health care provider, the number of visits allowed, or the length of time such coverage existed.

Subsequently, it was possible for insured persons to have wide variances of coverage specific to mental health treatment that differed from their coverage for physical health treatment. The same was true for the costs of mental health medications. The Mental Health Parity and Addiction Equity Act mandated that insurers must cover mental health visits at the same co-pay as they charge an insured patient for all other medical visits. The same became true for prescriptions for mental health drugs. The act was passed in 2008 under the George W. Bush administration. (Barry, Colleen L., etal. pp. 973–975.) https://pubmed.ncbi.nlm.nih.gov/27269016/

The "Stimulus" and Health Information Technology

In 2009, the Health Information Technology for Economic and Clinical Health (HITECH) Act as part of the American Recovery and Reinvestment Act of 2009 (ARRA) was signed. This act is fundamentally important because funding was now available to support electronic communication between physicians and specialties, while also reinforcing patient privacy and security. The act enabled patients to receive a summary care document upon discharge so that a patient knew exactly the care they received, what was the diagnosis, and what was prescribed for them. No longer would people complain they couldn't read the notes. An added benefit was that all prescriptions would be entered into the electronic medical record, thereby reducing patients' ability to request prescriptions from multiple physicians ("doctor-shopping").

President Barack Obama recognized The Patient Protection and Affordable Care Act - "Obamacare" - and the need for government intervention.

Benefits to Mental Health from the Affordable Care Act Passed in 2010

While the Patient Protection and Affordable Care Act (commonly known as ACA or, more casually, **Obamacare**) continues to be controversial, it has provided significant improvements in access to care for people with SMI. The ACA sought to offer insurance at affordable costs to individuals and families. Prior to its passage, sick people would often avoid seeking medical treatment, particularly if they had little disposable income.

Such a person might be forced to seek treatment in an emergency room as a last resort. Treatment in an emergency room is the most expensive form of outpatient medical treatment. As uninsured patients began to use emergency rooms, many hospitals were unable to seek financial reimbursement. The loss of emergency treatment revenue contributed to the closure of many hospitals nationwide, especially in small communities and in rural America.

The ACA plan was a comprehensive act implemented in various stages every other year for nearly 10 years. Incentives were offered to states if they chose to participate and expand Medicaid. *This act provided the first flow of federal dollars dedicated to mental health care since the 1980s.* Key features of the act that impacted mental health included:

• Parents could keep their children insured to age 26.

- Treatment for physical, mental, and addiction health issues would be integrated—that is they would be assessed and addressed for the same patient by the primary care provider.

- A role was acknowledged for the federal government in providing funding for prevention of and early intervention in mental illnesses.

- Medicaid plans and state-based insurance exchanges were required to cover behavioral health care.

- Pre-existing illness was excluded as a determinant for rate charges.

- Medicaid eligibility for low-income workers was expanded to reduce emergency room treatment (again prevention).

- Medicaid plans were required to cover preventive tests (such as cholesterol testing, mammograms, and diabetes testing).

- People with mental illness often had preventable diseases that went untreated, causing early deaths or permanent disabilities. Funding was provided for the recognition and treatment of mental illness (not to be confused with organic issues such as certain dementias of the older adult population). Organic mental health issues, such as stroke or physical accidents, are frequently differentiated because

their origin generally is a source other than psychiatric causes.

- Emphasis on Prevention and Wellness

For discussions on the impact of the ACA on Mental Health, see https://www.commonwealthfund.org/blog/2020/aca-10-how-has-it-impacted-mental-health-care (Mechanic and Mark Olfson, pp. 515–542.).

The bill provided for the **integration** of mental, physical, and addiction health. Previously mental and addiction health were addressed in separate departments at the federal, state, and local levels. Additionally, there were separate departments of alcohol abuse, again at the federal, state, and local levels. *The goal of integrated care was to introduce the concept of collaboration between the primary care physician and specialty treatment providers.* Various structures were created such as "medical homes" intended as patient-centered and Accountable Care Organizations (ACOs) to act as coordinators of care. Ideally a primary care provider could routinely assess for mental, physical, and substance abuse and determine appropri-ate referrals in a single office visit. (Barry & Huskamp)

How to Coordinate/Integrate Care

The organizations that volunteered to provide for the care, coordination, and management of patient care were often health maintenance organizations (HMOs). Originally expanded in

California under the Reagan gubernatorial administration, HMOs actually proved that **prevention worked**. Health maintenance organizations reasoned it would save costs if they provided early treatment of physical illnesses and/or tracked patients who had chronic illness by following up with them with regular appointments. Thus, HMOs charged a flat monthly fee for which their organization would provide a range of medical services, lab work, and prescriptions. While the best known is Kaiser Permanente, there are currently many HMOs with other health insurance companies. Contrary to popular beliefs, HMOs are not "socialized medicine." They are simply a different billing system for the provision of medical care.

Health maintenance organizations became a natural fit for offering additional plans under the ACA, particularly in part-nership with Medicare. A hybrid blossomed—the Medicare Advantage Plan. Details vary, but in general these hybrids offer a bundle of medical services that includes prescriptions, lab work, mental and addiction health care, and help with lifestyle modifi-cations such as smoking cessations and weight loss. The patient usually agrees to receive all of his/her medical care through the HMO network. This description is in no way intended to provide a detailed explanation of each and every HMO, but rather to give a general overview of how they work.

Note that the ACA is **not limited to low-income subscribers**. In general, there are four types or bands of coverage: bronze, silver, gold, and platinum. In general, the lower the co-pay, the lower the coverage. Conversely, higher costs provide more coverage with lower co-pays. There are people who, on careful examination of the coverage through ACA, have chosen to leave their employer-provided plan because of the more generous coverage and fixed annual cap. But for low-income workers, many of whom had no access to employer-sponsored insurance, the ACA provides financial **subsidies** to enable them to have coverage.

There have been and continue to be huge political and legal battles surrounding "Obamacare." The very last part of the ACA was rolled out in 2019. But, for those of us who are in some way connected with people with mental health issues, it has made a huge difference.

Other Important Influences

These bills came about as the result of many organizations advocating for many years. Grassroots organizations like the National Alliance on Mental Illness (NAMI) stand out because many of their members are family members, especially parents of adults with SMI. They braved stigma, advocated, organized, wrote letters, testified at hearings, and in general did whatever it took to ensure their loved ones received access to mental health care.

During the decades of annual budget cuts to mental health care funding, the peer advocacy model developed. This has resulted in mental health treatment being not only community-based but also based on the 12-step recovery model. This model borrowed from the philosophy followed by Alcoholics Anonymous and other related programs that asserts the medical model cannot help an alcoholic. Only one alcoholic talking to another can be effective. There are evolving changes in attitudes between staff members and persons with lived experiences as the voice of peers are included on mental health teams.The empowerment of the peer community is reflected in slogans such as "Nothing about us without us." Governor Newsom signed the bill to officially recognize the voice of people with Lived Experience (of Mental Illness) by creating a Peer Certification program. (CA State Senate Bill SB-803)

Medical Model vs Recovery Model (typical)

There have been tensions between the need for and use of medications for people who have Co-Occurring Disorders. Some people have both Serious Mental Illness and Substance Abuse issues. Under the medical model, a person is expected to seek a physician and possibly get prescriptions to alleviate their symptoms.

Many people in the addiction community reject the engagement of a doctor. Some advocates feel that a person is no longer sober if they're taking medications. While this has been a long-standing philosophical disagreement, Medication Assisted Therapy is a rapidly expanding treatment modality for persons who have both substance-abuse disorders and serious mental illness. Going forward, innovations such as neurofeedback may provide new modalities to treat SMI.

Summary

Despite the controversy surrounding the ACA, this piece of legislation provided for mental and addiction health issues to be addressed and funded. The ACA returns to the view that the federal government has a duty and a responsibility to serve people who have SMI and it provides an integrated model of treatment at an equitable rate. This is in contrast to the **fee-for-service model** of care that requires a patient to be seen for each medical problem on separate office visits.

Previously, mental health visits were often denied.

Often those policies that provided for mental health treatment had a cap of the total amount of care that could be accessed for the life of the claimant. Given that many forms of SMI can become chronic, especially if not treated early, the net effect was denial of mental health care to many young and older adults, often due to lack of desire to treat this population. While people may have refused mental health care due to the nature of their particular illness, prior to the passage of the Parity Act and the ACA, mental health care and psychiatric medications were "unavailable" because people often lacked the money to obtain them.

Author's Perspectives

The debates for the ACA's enactments were fraught with mistruths and rumors. There were several akin to following:

- People will have a chip implanted in their brains where government will track their movements

- Healthcare will be rationed

- Death squads for grandma

Big Brother is watching you from the book 1984

After 10 years of implementation, none of these have borne out. It is unfortunate that politicians have seized on the ACA with ferocious determination to destroy it without thoughtful discussions that might present improved policies rather than just to replace and repeal it. Many stakeholders with competing interests must be heard in order to create a cogent healthcare policy.

Can we do that? Of course we can! We can create anything we have the determination to do. It is up to us, however, to educate ourselves about mental health. Remember that mental health care providers, family members and its end users **must be included** in policy discussions about health care. Then we can decide how, or whether, we care enough to provide low-barrier access to quality mental health care services. Or will we simply continue to not provide treatment, refuse to pay taxes to help fund services, and pay more as people with untreated brain disease wander aimlessly on the streets of our cities, cycling between homelessness or housed in jails? The choice is ours!

This is an exciting time. Changes are already underway.

CHAPTER 4
STATE OF CARE IN CALIFORNIA: PAST-PRESENT-FUTURE

Important Legislation

California has passed landmark legislation regarding mental health. Most legislation for mental health springs from motivation to improve conditions for people affected with SMI. Legislation often has unforeseen and/or unintended consequences. Remember that all legislation is made by competing interest groups. This is part of our democracy. In mental health, for example, laws were passed to carve out special spaces for the treatment of people who suffer from SMI apart from being locked up in jails and prisons. Hospitals were created as a new, more humane setting where people could receive treatment, physical safety from abusive inmates and predatory staff members, and have a better quality of life.

Over time, however, psychiatric hospitals, especially publicly funded ones, became synonymous with phrases like "snake pits" or "lunatic asylum". They became viewed as unsafe places where the patients receive little treatment beyond warehousing and state-sanctioned medical treatments such as involuntary sterilizations and lobotomies.

After the Great Depression, especially following the return of veterans from World War II with significant levels of mental illness, questions mounted about the effectiveness of mental health treatment. At the federal level, the passage of the Community Mental Health Centers Act of 1963 was an attempt to assess the state of our mental health care system.

California also began to assess the condition of its mental health care system. The result of that investigation was the passage of the Short-Doyle Act (SD Act) in 1957. The SD Act provided local jurisdictions with a tool to establish mental health treatment services instead of sending residents to an institution located physically far away from their community. The state provided financial incentives to assist local governments— usually counties—in creating community mental health care programs, especially for the indigent population.

In 1967 the landmark Lanterman-Petris-Short (LPS) Act was passed. Prior to the passage of this legislation, there was no clearly defined path to obtain release from a psychiatric hospital. It was common for a person to remain in a state hospital far in excess of 20–40 years. If a patient also had court charges, the time spent in the hospital often was not counted toward satisfying any kind of prison sentence.

During the emerging movement to transfer chronic patients from the back "wards" of a state hospital into the community, **it was not unusual for me to move patients who had been admitted 30–40 years previously.** For example, in 1967, I moved a female patient out of the hospital into a community boarding house. She had been admitted in 1918. This was not uncommon. Nobody wanted these people returned to their communities—not their families, not the communities they came from, and especially not the hospital staff members, many of whom had long-term relationships with them.

Yet within the mental health community the mood was buoyant at that time, and filled with optimism. Patients were now given medications instead of electroshock or insulin shock treatments. New treatment modalities were instituted that allowed for patients to have a voice, such as patient self-government on hospital units. State hospitals had always functioned much like a closed community filled with specific pecking orders, both among staff members and among patients. Much of the labor done on the grounds such as gardening, cashiering in the canteen, and writing and editing the campus newsletter was done by patients. These jobs were often privileges the patients highly coveted.

The LPS Act brought a gradual end to the indeterminate sentencing into "snake pits."

Initially the patients transferred from the state hospital into the community were very institutionalized. They were placed in newly created state-sanctioned private homes located in a community. The need to wait for a hospital staff person with keys to approve exits from one's unit was eliminated. From the perspective of the patients there was an exhilarating sense of freedom of movement. They were also on "Leave of Absence" from the state hospital which could result in a return to the hospital. That legal designation meant that the patient was still connected to the state hospital.

Under the LPS Act, hospitals learned their new reality meant an end to Monday–Friday psychiatry. Treatment was expected to occur on weekends as well as legal holidays since there was now a clock ticking from the time the LPS Act 5150 Hold was instituted. (The LPS Act refers to Sections 5150, 5151, and 5152 of the Welfare and Institutions Code, a California law governing the involuntary civil commitment of individuals who due to mental illness pose a danger to self or others, or who are gravely disabled and require inpatient psychiatric care.)

The LPS Act influenced mental health legislation in other states. While not all states have a 72-hour hold, most states passed mental health legislation that clearly and legally defines a criterion for hospitalizing a person involuntarily. These new laws overwhelmingly tilted toward providing involuntary detention due to mental illness based on:

- Danger to self.

- Danger to others.

- "Gravely disabled," meaning the person cannot provide for their own food, clothing, etc. _as the result of their mental illness._

Since funding for public mental health care was effectively eliminated by the block grant program, the phrase "gravely disabled" often fell out of use despite a person's obvious need. Involuntary hospitalizations were frequently made on the basis of who was "most dangerous" due to the shortage of funding. Often front-line staff members felt they could get a person admitted to a prestigious university faster than they could get a person with active psychosis admitted to an inpatient hospital for mental health treatment. The impact on society, and especially on families, became devastating.

The Tarasoff Act (1976)

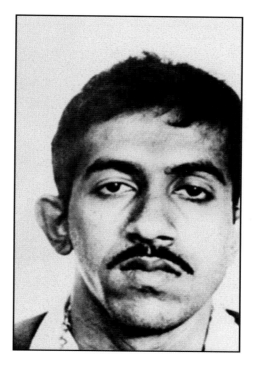

Prosenjit Poddar

Prior to the passage of the Tarasoff Act, therapists, much like priests and attorneys, were governed by rules holding that confidentiality between therapist and patient could be breached only under extreme circumstances. Many therapists and their agencies were reluctant to take action to warn people that a possible threat to their safety had been disclosed to the therapist.

While it might seem obvious to some, many therapists questioned whether such disclosures required them to predict the future—damaging the trust that exists within the therapeutic relationship with their client—or to determine how threats made in anger might actually just be outbursts.

Tatiana Tarasoff

Therapists Must Disclose

The Tarasoff Act was passed following a legal case involving unrequited love between an exchange student, Prosenjit Poddar, at the University of California, Berkeley, and a coed, Tatiana Tarasoff. The two met in September 1968 and dated briefly. While he apparently wanted an ongoing relationship, she stated she was interested in dating others. This precipitated a severe emotional crisis in Poddar sufficient for him to enter therapy, where he was diagnosed with schizophrenia. The treating therapist did report to the campus police that in his opinion Poddar was a danger. On questioning, however, Poddar was deemed mentally clear and was shortly released.

Later Poddar discontinued treatment, but befriended and moved in with Tatiana's brother. On October 27, 1969, he implemented the murder plan he had revealed to the therapist. Tatiana's parents subsequently sued the therapist and the university. While Poddar was convicted of second-degree murder in the first trial, there was a second trial in which the decision was that he would simply be required to return to his home country of India.

While the ethical implications for therapists continue to be debated in professional circles, the legal responsibility for therapists to break confidentiality if there is a danger to others was defined in the Tarasoff Act of 1976.

Laura's Law (2002)

Like many pieces of legislation, this legislation was enacted following a tragic death.

A volunteer in a California behavioral treatment facility, 19-year-old Laura Wilcox, was killed, along with others, by a person who had psychiatric symptoms and who had refused psychiatric treatment. The bill that became known as Laura's

Law sought to emulate New York's Kendra's Law. The bill, while passed in 2002, was not implemented until 2009 due to disputes about how it should be written. Additionally, each county could decide whether to offer such a program.

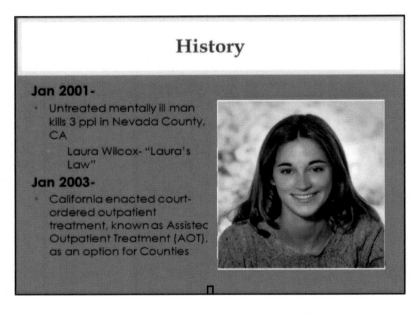

Excerpt from Laura's Law Presentation

Laura's Law is specifically designed to help individuals with mental illness who suffer from a condition known as "anosognosia," a complete lack of awareness of their mental illness. (California Association of Local Behavioral Health Board and Commissions) Like many pieces of legislation, this legislation was enacted following a tragic death. In 2020 Governor Newsom signed AB 1976, expanding Laura's Law throughout the state and removing any expiration date. (Symon, Evan 2020.)

What Is Laura's Law?

This law provides assisted outpatient treatment (AOT) for people who have SMI but who do not meet the rigorous standards to be hospitalized involuntarily. The law authorizes courts to order treatment if absolutely necessary. The intention of the legislation is to provide a bridge between the refusal of a person with symptoms (but who has observable negative impacts in their daily functioning) and the eventual acceptance of services. It *does not force people to take their medications,* but it does seek to engage with people and to interrupt the "revolving door" aspect of a small percentage of people who cycle in and out of emergency rooms, jails, and/or homelessness. Many people, especially family members, have expressed disappointment that the bill does not provide for forced (involuntary) medication treatment since they've experienced radical differences with their loved ones when they are/are not taking their medications. There is often a view that the primary treatment for their loved one is to simply resume taking their medications. (Tsai & Quanbeck Presentation)

People who have mental illness argue that *as adults they should retain the right to refuse medications*; and that in no other branch of medicine are patients forced to accept treatment, even with life-threatening illnesses. Cancer patients get to choose whether to engage in chemotherapy or other recommended treatments despite the fact that refusing might cause their death. One can choose to take insulin or not, recognizing the consequences may be dire.

Others argue that people who have SMI can present a danger to others. They argue that this distinguishes SMI from other medical conditions. Some legal scholars argue that there should be an actual assault to others, which would constitute a criminal act, and that until that crime has been committed, people have a right to refuse treatment, including medications.

__The issue of civil rights and the right to choose psychiatric treatment is often at the crux of mental health care policy and mental health debates.__

Proposition 63 (The Millionaires' Tax) (2004)

By 2004, a broad consensus was reached among California voters that the needs of people with SMI *had* to be addressed. Since federal funding for mental health care had been decimated by the block grant solution in the 1980s, services to adults who suffered from serious and observable mental health symptoms had largely devolved into only providing hospitalization to the most severely affected. Often the LPS Act was only applied to people who were a danger to self or others. Gravely disabled people often fell by the wayside due to lack of funding. No longer was this a problem for family members alone. Business owners, tourists, law enforcement personnel, and the community at large had begun to feel the impact of the obvious lack of services. It was in this climate that Senator Darrell Steinburg authored

Proposition 63, the Mental Health Services Act, which passed in 2004.

What Does Proposition 63 Provide?

- More than 3 million adults are affected by potentially disabling mental illnesses every year in California. (Karen George & Patrick Ma)

- Proposition 63 emphasizes transformation of the mental health care system with the **intention of expanding services** while improving the quality of life for Californians living with or at risk of SMI.

- Proposition 63 is funded by levying a percent tax on personal income over $1 million.

The legislation provides very specific functions:

- Community Services and Supports (CSS) provides for direct services to individuals who have SMI.

- Capital Facilities and Technological Needs (CFTN) provides for projects including improvement or buildings and increasing technological capacity.

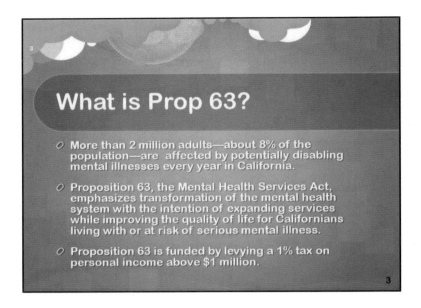

What is Prop 63?

○ More than 2 million adults—about 8% of the population—are affected by potentially disabling mental illnesses every year in California.

○ Proposition 63, the Mental Health Services Act, emphasizes transformation of the mental health system with the intention of expanding services while improving the quality of life for Californians living with or at risk of serious mental illness.

○ Proposition 63 is funded by levying a 1% tax on personal income above $1 million.

3

- Workforce, Education, and Training (WET) provides for building and/or increasing the capacity to provide trained staff members.

- Prevention and Early Intervention (PEI) provides for training for families or providers to recognize and treat early signs of mental illness.

- Innovation (INN) provides funding and evaluation for new approaches to the delivery of mental health care services, promotes interagency collaboration, and recognizes culturally appropriate ways of providing access to treatment in underserved communities.

Note that a portion of the revenues must be invested in **brain research** annually. Two institutes, named for Senator Steinberg, were established: University of California Davis and University of California Los Angeles.

The legislation specifically restricts the amount of funding that can be used for administrative costs and previously existing programs and expenses. An oversight structure was included in the bill. Provisions with an emphasis on consumer and family participation are:

- Age-specific needs.

- Cultural competence.

- Outcomes and accountability must include clients.

- Reduce stigma.

Here are some of the programs that were created as the result of the Millionaire's Tax:

- Treatment of first-time psychosis with the goal of preventing a second episode or a lifetime of it.

- Treatment for children 0–5 years old.

- Intensive treatment for young adults age 16–26.

- Co-location of mental health services in settings such as community colleges, senior centers, welfare departments, and courts.

- Outreach mental health programs to engage community residents in increasing awareness of mental health issues and reducing stigma.

- Growth of non-traditional treatment modalities (non-pharmacological).

- Return to brain research.

- Reduction of resistance by addiction medicine practitioners to accept medications as sometimes desirable (medication-assisted treatment).

Realignment Bill (AB 109) (2011)

In order to comply with court-ordered mandates to reduce overcrowding in state prisons, AB 109 was passed in 2011. The bill provided for the transfer of nonserious, nonviolent, non-sex-offenders to be transferred to county-operated jails. The prisoners often remained segregated from the local county jail population. In anticipation of the process of identifying the demographics of these prisoners, some counties established teams that included mental health professionals. It became clear that many of those prisoners had committed crimes due to their untreated mental health and/or substance abuse issues.

Thus, in an effort to prevent recidivism on parole, these counties engaged with prisoners prior to release to assist them with reintegration into community life. The impact of AB 109 has included:

- Rapid decline of prison population.

- Prison sentences declining to pre-1977 levels.

- Vast disparity in county responses.

- Unprecedented expansion of community-based corrections.

- Momentum for further reforms. (Center on Juveniles and Criminal Justice)

Investment in Mental Health Wellness Act (SB 82) (2013)

While Proposition 63 provided for the funding of mental health care services, a gap was identified in seeking to provide them. Specifically, in order to implement some of the services (such as community-based psychiatric urgent care centers, crisis residential treatment, and mobile crisis support teams), space was needed to house them. Therefore, the Investment in Mental Health Wellness Act was passed in 2013. The construction of facilities in local communities was seen as a down payment towards reducing more costly inpatient hospitalizations.

Senator Darrell Steinberg, Author of Proposition 63 and SB 82

LPS Conservatorship

A Word about Conservatorship

California laws provide for involuntary mental health treatment only under certain circumstances. The criteria are spelled out in the Lanterman Petris Short Act, and is the legal term used in California which gives one adult (conservator) the responsibility for overseeing the comprehensive medical treatment for an adult (conservatee) who has a serious mental illness. (NAMI. org) There are several levels of requirements that must be met in order to obtain a conservatorship. At each level, the requirements of evidence increase. If the person has improved, they may "no longer meet criteria". The conservatorship proceedings end at that point.

Level 1: Welfare and Institutions Code 5150.

A duly authorized mental health practitioner certifies that the patient is a danger to him/herself or to others, or is gravely disabled and needs to be placed in a psychiatric hospital for up to 72 hours for evaluation and treatment. A person might have obvious thought disorders that may not rise to the level of threat (to self or others).

*[**Author note:** This is where a lot of family tension lives. If the loved one does not meet criteria to be placed on a hold, this invites confusion and frustration among the family members who took the risk to call 911. "What does "**NOT** meeting criteria"*

mean? Can't they see that he needs HELP?" This can be very damaging to the family dynamics in general. It may also place elderly parents in danger.]

Level 2: Welfare and Institutions Code 5250

The person is provided an attorney and informed of his/her rights, including the right to have a hearing and to be represented by an attorney. Psychiatric staff members present evidence or *probable cause* to believe the person's mental disorder rises to the level of threat to others or self, or is a grave disability. Treatment is recommended for an additional 14 days.

Level 3: Welfare and Institutions Code 5352.3

Psychiatric hospital staff members can hold the person for an additional 3 days to allow for the filing of request for a conservatorship proceeding.

Level 4: Welfare and Institutions Code 5270.55

Psychiatric hospital staff members can detain and treat the person for an additional 30 days without filing for a temporary conservatorship not to exceed 47 days.

Level 5: Welfare and Institutions Code 5300

Psychiatric hospital staff members can detain and treat a person involuntarily for 180 days if there is risk to others, actual or threatened. Often families are introduced to the concept of a conservatorship for their loved one with little information about the process or how it may impact their lives or the lives of their loved one.

- A conservatorship may be granted of the person, the estate, or both.

- Conservatorship should not be confused with power of attorney.

- Conservatorship is awarded for a maximum of 1 year. It must be renewed annually.

- The person must be provided legal counsel.

- ***Probate conservatorship*** is a different type of conservatorship.

- A public agency usually conducts an investigation prior to the hearing.

- Often the conservatorship process has a priority to name the conservator.

  Family members have priority to be named conservators. Under certain circumstances a third party may be named such as the county Office of Public Guardian or private agent. See *www.courts.ca.gov/documents/handbook.pdf* for a handbook that explains conservatorship in greater detail. Additionally, free classes in the community are available to families that present detailed 62 information about the conservatorship process by such groups as the National Alliance on Mental Illness (NAMI). (Abrams, Time Magazine)

Things to Ponder

Many stakeholders are involved in the battle regarding involuntary mental health treatment:

- Organizations that advocate against involuntary treatment, especially medications.

- Organizations that offer protections against the abuse of vulnerable adults.

- Organizations that provide access to treatment, even if involuntary, as a methodology to assist the patient in regaining mental stability.

- Organizations that seek to retain locking up people who have SMI for profit.

Increasingly the trend is away from hospitalizations. There has been a shift away from access to treatment from government and private hospitals to families.

Here are some trends to watch for:

- Crisis stabilization treatment units are becoming more commonly available. They are community-based, open 24 hours, and allow for observation/treatment without the cost of in-patient hospitalization.

- Peer certification programs.

- Many states have begun incorporating adults with "lived experience" on treatment teams who serve adults with serious and persistent forms of mental illness. (California passed a similar act that went into effect January 1, 2021.) Community networks are also growing of people with such lived experience. These have various names and may be linked to mental health organizations, neighborhood groups, faith-based groups, and/or support groups for specific diagnoses. These groups are not therapy groups, so participants may feel more comfortable since no staff is documenting.

- Psychiatric Assisted Directive (PAD). This tool is becoming more widely used by people with lived experience. The person who has mental illness creates a document while stable in which he/she indicates who they want involved, for what functions, in the event of relapse.

- Law enforcement and mental health personnel are increasing their utilization of mental health practitioners to take the lead on 911 calls involving mental health. A new three-digit telephone code – 988 – has recently been funded by Gov. Newsom that will

be dedicated to mental health calls. (Calmatters.
org)

- Community housing increasingly includes permanent, onsite supportive services.

- There is an increasing use of injectable long-acting
pharmaceuticals, which allows a person to avoid
multiple daily dosing of medications.

- Proposed revision of the LPS Act.

These are but a few of the exciting changes in providing
services to adults who have serious and persistent forms of
mental illness.

Summary

The current California governor, Gavin Newsom, has spoken
publicly about the need to provide support for services to young
and older adults suffering from SMI. He has taken steps to study
the current status of mental health services to this population in
all 58 counties of California. He has also demonstrated that he
is listening to families and end users of the public mental health
system. He has personally visited licensed Adult Residential
Facilities (board-and-care homes) for adults who are low-income
and who have Serious Mental Illness. During his visits, he spent
considerable time with the residents learning why they valued
living in a board-and-care home.

Supporting licensed board-and-care homes for people with SMI has been a long-standing passion and point of my personal advocacy. It is encouraging to see monies dedicated to these board-and-care homes in the 2021 California state budget. People who have SMI often benefit from the services licensed facilities provide such as:

- Three meals daily plus snacks.

- Maximum of two people per room.

- Housekeeping.

- 24-hour staff members.

- Medication management and administration.

Because these facilities currently receive a rate of almost $45.00 per diem, many are closing. I am very encouraged by the actions the governor, as well as the various coalitions statewide, and of course in my home county, the Los Angeles County Board of Supervisors, have taken to salvage this essential service. While not all people with Serious Mental Illness need the structure of a board-and-care facility, it can provide valuable service - especially to people who have recently experienced a psychotic episode.

These services often provide a bridge between acute illness and more independent lifestyles. They also provide a level of security to the community as well as a reduction in the use of emergency services such as hospital emergency rooms or arrests. (Wisner, Jonathan October 2021.) Currently, we are continuing to see homes close statewide. Failure to close this gap will result in facilities that are completely unregulated and that lack consumer protections such as a 30-day eviction policy. ***Note that most homes such as "independent homes" or "sober living homes" are not regulated by the state.***

While there could be a rate of $150 per diem with additional reimbursements for extra services for people who have complex issues such as addiction or physical illness, at the very least the rate of reimbursement should mirror the rate paid by the state to facilities that have the same license and who serve Adults who have Intellectual Disabilities. Otherwise, it would appear that there is a ***Disparity in Services*** to populations. Given the advances the Newsom administration has made, I have reason to hope for an overhaul of our state mental health system.

CHAPTER 5
THE IMPACT OF SERIOUS MENTAL ILLNESS ON FAMILIES

The impact of living with any family member who has a long-term illness or disability has certain characteristics. The Kubler-Ross model of the five stages of grief following the loss of a life—denial, anger, bargaining, depression, and acceptance—in some respects can be easily applied to families who love a family member with a disability. If it's a mental disability, the effects can be staggering due to the unpredictability of the illness itself. (Kubler-Ross)

The Five Stages

Stage 1: Denial

Denial takes many forms. I've often heard:

- He's not slow. He's actually quite smart!

- This probably happened because he's been hanging out with the wrong crowd.

- We think somebody put a drug in his drink/soft drink and it made him act crazy.

- I think he had a crush on a girl. She broke his heart and it's making him a little off-kilter.

The family members view this behavior as out of the norm for their loved one. They are looking for an explanation for the irrational behavior. They're looking for clues, and that may include looking at peers, daily activities, text messages, and the level of outside stress. It is their expectation that this is a single occurrence and that with proper treatment this kind of behavior will never happen again.

Parallel Process

Parents don't realize their adult child is going through this same process as he/she struggles to understand what has transpired.

- Maybe somebody drugged their drink/food or tried to poison them. Maybe they shouldn't eat any food they didn't personally prepare because whoever wants to kill them may be secretly poisoning their food or maybe they've put ground glass in the food so that he/she might slowly bleed to death undetected.

- Maybe some powerful person has taken control of their mind.

- Maybe they're no good and don't deserve to live.

- Maybe God is speaking to them or wants them to die because their faith isn't strong enough.

After the initial crisis has been abated, both the identified patient (the one who has now entered mental or behavioral health treatment) and the parents are often in a state of shock. As they breathe a collective sigh of relief that the hospitalization or crisis is over, all parties are certain their lives can now return to normal. That might mean returning to college or to whatever vocational path they were on. *All is well.*

Stage 2: Anger

Around the third episode the family members begin to wonder what they did wrong. By now they may have experienced some anger:

- Anger at the identified patient.

- Anger at the mental health professionals who have not truly "fixed" the problem.

- Anger at the other parent as they seek to find out which parent has mental illness in their family tree. *The blame game begins.*

- Anger at the disruption of the normal routine due to the reemergence of psychosis.

- Anger at the time one has to spend chasing resources.

- Anger at the patient—often unexpressed—from siblings as they watch the drama repeat and repeat and repeat.

- Anger at the many hours spent waiting—for the doctor to call, for the psychiatric emergency team to evaluate the adult child. Family members may hope the neighbors don't notice. What must the neighbors think with the paramedics and the police car?

- Anger at the notion that their life is now controlled by episodes that induce shame and guilt. *How long is this going to last? What will happen to my adult child if I die? Who will be there to look after him/her?*

The anger often must remain unexpressed. Who can they turn to? Mostly no one. And after all the drama, they still have to show up for work or school the next day as though nothing happened, often on little sleep. Anger and exhaustion become the norm.

Parallel Process

He's so frustrated!

Author Note: *At the same time the adult child is also feeling angry and frustrated.*

Stage 3: Bargaining

Over time, both the family members and the identified patient engage in a form of bargaining.

- Maybe if you take your medications none of this will ever happen again.

- Maybe we should look for some form of financial support. Just until you find a job/return to school/get on your feet.

- I read about a new medication that has wonderful effects. Maybe we should try it.

Since the ACA, adult children can stay on their parents' health insurance policy until age 26. *But what is going to happen after that? SSI/SSDI. What does that mean? Does that mean my beautiful child is disabled? Incurable? My child is not disabled. I will not agree to having my child be labeled. He/she is beautiful and smart and funny. I do not agree he/she has a mental disability.*

A bargain is struck. In order to have health insurance, the disability process is begun. Such a confusing maze of broken human beings. Some with obvious physical disabilities. Wheelchairs, walkers, service animals, mothers with new babies crying. They're probably there to get social security cards for their babies. Smiling at the memories of their adult child when life was simpler and their child was a baby, then a toddler, then school age.

The bargain requires revisiting painful memories in detail. Questions about medical, mental health treatment history must be answered.

Typical Parental Thought Process: *When was the first time it happened? Who was that doctor? Was it the second time or the first time that we had to drop everything and go up to the university and get him/her to a private psychiatric hospital? Oh yes, I remember now. It was all so painful I guess I blocked it out of my memory.*

In addition to questions about medical and mental health treatment history come questions about work history.

Typical Parental Thought Process: *No, he/she has never held a job for more than a few months. But he/she wants to work. We're here to apply because he's going to need health coverage so that he can see a doctor because after his next birthday he will no longer be covered on my plan. He does not want to be on disability. Of course I'll be his payee because he does not manage money very well. Besides, I'm already paying all of his bills anyway. So, I guess I will get a little bit of reimbursement.*

Stage 4: Depression

Depression wears many faces

Typical Parental Thought Process: *Depression. I don't know whether I'm depressed. I just no longer want to get out of bed. I am just so exhausted. I have to keep going, I know. But it's very hard. I jump when I hear the phone ring because I don't know who it might be. Maybe the police. You know we never had trouble with the police in my family. Now I'm involved with the police and court appearances all the time. I've got no more sick leave on my job because of taking off to take him to court, doctor appointments, applying for general relief or food stamps. It's always something. I used to never get sick. I've never even used my sick leave for me. Now I should actually go see a doctor about my (fill in the blank), but I have no sick time left. Now I can't afford to take time to see a doctor for myself.*

I don't sleep well. I keep thinking of what I could have done differently as a parent. It must be my fault somehow. Is God punishing me for loving him so much? Maybe I had too much pride in my son and God is making me get right-sized. I just don't see my future, either for me or for him. I'm not giving up. I'm just so very tired.

Stage 5: Acceptance

Acceptance is the final stage. The family members have begun to recognize that this is a recurring experience as they have careened from episode to episode. Through late-night emergency calls, clinics, hospitals with locked units, and partial hospital programs, they feel like a bumper car. They have now begun to recognize patterns like so many darkening clouds before a storm. They have surrendered. They are no longer looking for the reason *why* in the exterior environment. They get it. This is an internal problem outside of their ability to control or fix. They have tried many solutions but none have permanently restored their son/daughter to who they once were.

Perhaps their child is also weary from the roller coaster that is SMI, especially forms of schizophrenia.

Typical Parental Thought Process: *What is to become of their adult child? What kind of future will he/she have? Does this mean they will never host a wedding? Will there be no grandchildren? What happens to the dreams they had when their child was born and their promises to that infant that they would be the best parent they could possibly be? What happens to those dreams?*

Parents, especially mothers, need therapy to help them to process their feelings of failure, guilt, and shame. Perhaps then they can begin to see that while their adult child might be unable to achieve those original dreams, perhaps, with support and neutral third-party mental health resources, their child can create a healthy, purposeful life. While different, it can be a great life. In much the way injured workers often cannot return to their previous occupation, people can and do recreate themselves.

Note that while these stages of grief appear in a sequential order, in real life that is likely not to be the case. People can and often do fluctuate between stages. What's critical is that parents recognize they have needs of their own. Absent from this discussion is an underlying fear often experienced by elderly parents when cohabitating with their adult child. Most parents are loath to admit this fear even to themselves - that they are afraid of their own child. Failure to address this fear in a safe environment can have detrimental consequences. (The Spotlight Team, Boston Globe)

We must provide a safe environment that protects both adults with SMI and their parents. Parents need to be able to ask for help without risking that such a call might result in their adult child being shot to death or permanently disabled by law enforcement officials.

Protections for Parents

Parents, especially mothers, will frequently feel unable to have their child with mental disabilities live away from them. This often involves a combination of reasons.

- The adult child refuses to leave the home, particularly with certain co-occurring illnesses.

- The adult child refuses to engage with mental health resources because he/she too is in denial that he/she has any sort of mental illness.

Additionally, like most Americans, they have internalized stigma toward people with mental illness and do not want to be associated with such a group. Many people with SMI prefer to be incarcerated because it's more acceptable to them to be in jail than thought of as having a "mental problem." Others may choose to identify as an alcoholic and become regular members of Alcoholics Anonymous despite the fact that they have no substance abuse issues. The community and the stigma of being an alcoholic is preferable to being identified as a person with SMI.

Siblings

In families with multiple adult children and/or grandchildren, the siblings may object to including the identified patient in their current lives. Holiday gatherings, normally thought of as a time of inclusiveness, may force parents to choose. Adult siblings may refuse to have their own children "exposed to their crazy uncle." This further widens the sense of responsibility and isolation of the parent of the adult child with SMI. A parent may feel forced to decline a holiday meal with one adult child and his/her family (including the grandchildren) in order to be present for an adult child with SMI.

Often parents assume that upon their death, one of the other adult children will take responsibility for the identified patient. Often the other siblings have huge reservoirs of unexpressed rage toward the parent(s). They have witnessed the lion's share of the family's resources (time, energy, money, attention) given to the identified patient. The siblings often have had no individual or family therapy to help them process their own feelings of anger, perceived neglect, or favoritism.

They do not know these are normal feelings many people have if they have had a sibling with a chronic mental or physical disability. Since the advent of HIPAA and privacy laws, nearly all mental health treatment has focused almost entirely on the identified patient. Treatment modalities such as family therapy have fallen out of favor. The introduction of managed care and the limitation of the number of therapy sessions health insurance covers has also served to reduce the voices of siblings.

Living in Domestic Violence

Parents do a grave injustice to their adult children when they fail to set firm limits or insist they reside outside the home. Not only does it allow the adult children to perpetuate their belief that they are somehow different from other people with mental health issues, but it deprives them of acquiring the very life skills needed to survive once the parents have died.

As parents age they become more frail. They may place their own physical and mental safety at risk when they act as the *Representative Payee* (see glossary) for their adult child's disability benefits, especially if their loved one has co-occurring disorders. There may be monthly disputes with demands on the parent to provide funds to their loved one. Often the funds have already been given. In order to keep the peace, the parent gives additional money out of their own retirement funds.

Mom, the representative payee

Her Adult son, who does not remember receiving his money from mom. What does she do?

The parent is actually living in a situation of domestic violence. Since it's a parent/child relationship and not a romantic one, this form of domestic violence is often not recognized by Adult Protective Services (APS). Additionally, APS practices differ widely within the same county and across the state. For example, in some APS departments, each call is investigated to substantiate whether the charge is justified. If the charge is substantiated, the legal process automatically begins. In other APS departments, the practice is to require the aging parent to sign a complaint in order for there to be a legal filing. Some APS departments will investigate but will not proceed if the parent is above a certain income guideline or has a savings account with funds set aside to pay property taxes. Unfortunately for the aging parent, the other siblings are thoroughly disgusted with the parent(s) weak boundaries, so they refuse to engage. This serves to further isolate the aging parent.

One solution would be for the State of California to establish a Trust Office that could act as the representative payee. Professional fiduciaries rarely take these cases since little to no money could be paid for their services. There are a few not-for-profit organizations the state could contract with as an alternative to providing the service directly.

So Where Are We Now?

We are currently living with the outcomes of the Reagan mental health policy. The book **American Psychosis** sums the Reagan Philosophy thusly:

> *"President Reagan never understood mental illness. Like Richard Nixon, he was a product of the Southern California culture that associated psychiatry with Communism…. Reagan was also exposed to the consequences of untreated mental illness through the two sons of Roy Miller, his personal tax advisor. Both sons developed schizophrenia; one committed suicide in 1981, and the other killed his mother in 1983. Despite such personal exposure, **Reagan never exhibited any interest in the need for research or better treatment for serious mental illness.** [emphasis mine]"*

https://www.salon.com/2013/09/29/ronald_
reagans_shameful_legacy_violence_the_
homeless_mental_illness/ (Excerpted from
the book)

The alleged Reagan philosophy consisted of the following basic tenets:

- Families should be responsible for their adult children who have SMI. No taxpayer funds should be spent.

- No specialized training is necessary to work with people who have SMI. All you need is common sense. *[*Author note: This was an observed casual statement witnessed as a CA state employee. There is no available citation for this.]*

- There is no such thing as prevention because mental health professionals cannot prove that their intervention was the actual defining moment that caused a person to change a behavior. (It could've been a random comment from a stranger, for example.)

What have been the results of that treatment philosophy to families?

The impact and stress on families has been significant. It has caused untold mental health problems within families and even divorce between parents. The lack of funding for public mental health infrastructure has resulted in:

- Increase in homelessness of people with mental illness.

- Increase in incarceration of people with mental illness.

- Increase in community resistance toward including people with mental problems.

- Increase in self-medication and substance abuse as a way to self-manage psychosis.

- Limited mental health services have resulted in treatment going to only the most severely affected. This has resulted in generations of adults with SMI being denied access to early treatment of their psychosis. Today, there is evidence that early treatment of psychosis can prevent the development of chronic mental illness. Denial of treatment has meant not only lost happy lives, but potentially loss of tax revenues as they may have been able to enter the workforce.

- Increased injuries to and deaths of staff members in mental health treatment units.

- Increased levels of family stress, especially high levels of anxiety and depression.

- Increased levels of deadly force directed at first-degree family members.

- Increased levels of erroneous law enforcement shootings of people with SMI. (Sherin, & Stern (2020). LA Times)

Positive Outcomes of the Lack of Funding

Adaptation of the Recovery Model

Due to the annual cuts to mental health services, public mental health organizations began to recognize and increase the use of peers with "lived experience." Adaptation of the slogans from Alcoholics Anonymous such as "One alcoholic talking to another alcoholic" began to be transposed into the mental health slogan "Nothing about us without us."

Advocacy

We have seen organizations such as Treatment Advocacy Center, Mental Health America, and the NAMI begin to speak out publicly about the need for adults with SMI to get treatment. NAMI offers free education to family members to help them understand SMI and practical steps they can take. Parents have begun to testify in legislative hearings. They have openly advocated for increased tax-supported services for their adult children. This might have contributed to reducing stigma in the following ways:

- Increased public discussion around the lack of services for adults with SMI.

- Does not discriminate between private and public mental health systems

Summary and Author Perspective

If you're trying to figure out just how we got into such a mess in mental health—with or without homelessness—look no further than the presidential election of Governor Reagan from California. When he repealed (overturned) the Mental Health Systems Act of 1980 (Public Law 96-398) and instituted block grants instead, that was the silver bullet. Many problems that communities across the nation are experiencing, whether Houston, Chicago, Miami, Louisville, San Francisco, or, of course, Los Angeles, can be directly traced to the federal decision (Congressional) to withdraw funding earmarked for adults with SMI. The data, whether academic or in the media, show this correlation to be true. (Spotlight Team, Boston Globe)

If we don't mind having people wander the streets, often in deranged states, so we can have lower taxes, that is a choice. (Sherin, & Stern (2020). LA Times) I believe as Americans, we know we can do better. We have the skill sets to provide top-notch services. What if this is your son or daughter? Your sister or brother? Does that change your willingness to pay a few dollars more in federal taxes so they can have housing and meaningful purpose plus supportive services? What do you believe we as a country should do to resolve this problem?

Do you believe it is a problem? Ultimately this is a question of political will. (Sherin, & Stern (2020). LA Times).

CHAPTER 6

UNDERSTANDING SERIOUS MENTAL ILLNESS AS A MEDICAL DISABILITY

Historically, persons who have SMI have clearly demonstrated significant differences in how their brains process data. Yet, both in public policy and among private health insurers there has often been a reluctance to accept the notion that SMI is a disability. If a person is in a wheelchair, their medical disability is readily apparent both to the affected person and to observers. This is frequently not the case for persons who have SMI. There are even political advocacy groups who advocate for people with disabilities. Yet these same groups often "forget" to include people who have SMI.

The Impact of Having Mental Illness in Our History

For centuries in Western culture, including in the United States, many families have hidden mental illness, fearing such information might ruin marriage prospects for daughters or even cause deaths by mobs. The observed reality that there might be a genetic component has influenced some religions to recognize mental illness as a legitimate reason to terminate a marriage, even a long-term marriage with children. (Mooney, The Providence Journal)

In this author's experience, one of the common diagnoses I encountered as a young state hospital social worker in the late 1960s was involutional psychosis. Symptoms for this diagnosis included "agitation and depression, self-condemnation, hopelessness and a tendency toward hypochondriasis" (HustonPE, Locher LM.). Keep in mind, nearly all psychiatrists were cis (cisgender) men, and they were evaluating women. (Author's note: This diagnosis no longer exists.) This diagnosis was curious to me because it seemed to be only given to women, often in midlife.

It was fairly common for a well-heeled, successful man to drag his wife in for a psychiatric evaluation, citing her behavior as "crazy." The wife would be hospitalized for an indeterminate length of time. When the wife was finally discharged, perhaps years later, she would find that her husband had filed for divorce (insanity was one of the grounds for divorce acceptable even to religious authorities). He would also have sole custody of the children, all financial assets, and a new, younger wife. In 2020, I did not encounter anyone given that diagnosis. How this diagnosis may have been used to deprive long-married women of their rights is outside the scope of this work. Material is available, including academic journals as well as popular literature, if one is interested in studying that topic. *(See list in Phyllis Chesler, Women and Madness (1972); and Laura D. Hirshbein, Gender, Age, and Diagnosis: The Rise and Fall of Involutional Melancholia in American Psychiatry (1900–1980).)*

The first legislation allowing no-fault divorce was passed only in 1970. (California). Various states had divorce laws that permitted a divorce only if one of the spouses could be proven to have broken one of the laws allowing for a legal divorce. In some states, one of those grounds was mental illness.

Psychiatric diagnoses today are guided by a list of clearly observable symptoms as described in the DSM. The current publication is the fifth edition, so you may hear clinicians refer to DSM-5-TR. These classifications are used by clinicians, health insurance companies, nearly all mental health agencies in California and across America.

Serious mental illness is a medical problem that often interferes with a person's ability to achieve their full potential. It is sometimes called brain disease. Therefore, it is deserving of some form of financial, housing, vocational subsidy and access to quality mental health treatment.

This notion remains controversial. Many people still believe "he's not crazy all the time, so he can work full-time," or "he's just acting crazy."

Additionally, cultural and religious beliefs, myths, and laws often reflect a bias against helping an "able-bodied" person, despite clear and present demonstrated episodes of SMI. This is often called "blaming the victim." Films have also played a part in creating the belief that people with SMI are dangerous.

Moreover, in public policy, health insurers and even political advocacy groups, there is a reluctance to accept the concept of SMI as a disability. This lack of acceptance has generated a sense of "stigma" around mental illness for the affected person as well as their families. Families often kept their loved one hidden away. Psychosis was sometimes used as the justification for a husband to involuntarily hospitalize his wife (for an indeterminate length of time) or for terminating a marriage. These, and other factors, have often led families to hide mental illness. Some families actually go to great lengths and great expense such as avoiding the use of health insurance so that there's no "paper trail" of their loved one's mental illness. Some families hide family members from sight and use such strategies as keeping their family member locked in a room with meals served 3 times a day. Stigma remains a huge barrier to treatment

Times Are Changing:

Fortunately, there are signs that this sense of "stigma" applied to SMI is diminishing. Employers are acknowledging "mental health" days off as acceptable sick days. Celebrities and sports figures are sharing their own mental health challenges. (https://invisibledisabilities.org/) Still, stigma continues to prevent changes in public policy that would provide better and comprehensive services in the community. We, as a nation, continue to struggle with the conflicting ideas of providing mental health services versus admitting that we have mental health needs for those services.

Author's Notes:

In hindsight, we can observe how the attitudes, beliefs, and values of a culture can be used to define mental illness. We can view the burning of so-called witches, the use of leeches to cure diseases, the shunning of people thought to be possessed by demons or other practices as barbaric/backwards. We are certain that in our modern culture, WE would never be guilty of such judgmental attitudes. We are certain that we would never base medical treatment, mental health treatment or laws on unfounded, unscientific information. We are certain that we will only use "Evidence-Based" information. Our decisions will always be based upon data.

Yet stigma continues to be widespread. Beliefs that "demons" are the cause of hearing voices continue to be widespread.

We must continue to shine bright light on Serious Mental Illness. We must fund independent research so that someday we might have a vaccine against these brain diseases that rob so many wonderful young people of living the lives they thought they would live. This change is within our grasp—if only we would grab it. Make it better for the next generations.

Summary

Historically, in public policy, health insurers and even political advocacy groups, there is a reluctance to accept the concept of SMI as a disability. This lack of acceptance has generated a sense of "stigma" around mental illness for the affected person as well as their families.

Today, there are signs that this sense of "stigma" applied to SMI is diminishing. Celebrities and sports figures are sharing their own mental health challenges. Hopefully these celebrities will encourage everyday people to ask for help.

CHAPTER 7
THE FINANCING OF MENTAL HEALTH

Understanding Social Security Insurance

Social Security Administration Seal

While the financing of mental health treatment may be managed by public laws requiring school districts to provide appropriate education for all school-aged children, parents quickly learn that once their child "ages out" of the school district or off their health insurance, they are frequently faced with dismay, confusion, and even a certain level of quiet panic. Part of this confusion is the lack of clarity given to families about this essential piece of the financial puzzle

What is the difference between SSI and SSDI? This chapter addresses the broad differences between the two programs. *In no way is this description intended to replace the advice available at your local Social Security Administration. It is <u>always</u> advisable to seek direction about your specific case.*

<u>Always talk to Social Security directly.</u>

General Information

Supplemental Security Income

- Apply via the Social Security Administration.

   o Start with a telephone call: **800-772-1213**.

   o There may be a substantial wait time, but it is worth it to speak to a live person rather than applying online.

- There will be considerable paperwork to complete, including a form documenting observed behaviors/ limitations by a third party who knows the claim-ant well.

- There is no apportionment of fault. The claimant has only two criteria to consider:

   o Is the person disabled under the Social Security guidelines?

- o Is this disability covered by the Social Security Administration?

- There is no such thing as "Partially Disabled," although there are provisions for returning to work.

- Specific financial guidelines are required for approval of the applicant. SSI is federally mandated with a cap of $2000.00 in assets for a single individual. Fortunately, California has decided to eliminate that policy effective January 2024.

- Once approved, health insurance is attached: Medicaid aka MediCal.

- Once approved, the claimant may become eligible for other funding. However, requests for such approvals cannot be determined without the claimant first being approved as a person with a disability.

Social Security Disability Insurance

Social Security Disability Insurance (SSDI) is one of the stated reasons for the existence of social security within the Social Security Act. Social Security legislation provides insurance coverage for participating employers/employees for old age, survivors and disability (OASDI). Thus, eligibility is based on contributions paid in by the claimant, usually within a fixed amount of time preceding the date of application.

Note: Eligibility is not based on the total number of years the claimant has paid into the fund, unlike old age pension funds.

Example: John Doe, age 37, applies for SSDI. His claim is denied. Why? While John has been working off and on since his late teens in the construction industry, due to his disability and his belief that he could still work, John has only worked for a few weeks at a time for the past eight years as a "walk-on" to construction sites. He was paid cash on those sites and was never made an employee. He did not pay into Social Security.

If the claimant is found to be disabled within the definitions of SSD law, the claimant is approved. This fund will be used before SSI since SSI is public money.

- Notice that both applications are processed by the Social Security Administration

The Medical Insurance that accompanies **SSDI** is **Medicare.** Unfortunately, despite the fact that a claimant is found to be disabled, there is now a 2-year wait period in order for the Medicare to begin. Some or all of the 24-month waiting period may be absorbed by the length of time the application takes to get approved. Payment is retroactive to the date of application. If the case has gone to the hearing level, often the wait time for the hearing exceeds the 24-month Medicare wait time. While the claimant may be required to wait for Medicare, they will likely be eligible for MediCal (Medicaid).

Author's Note: If you live outside the state of California, because states vary, it is always necessary to talk to your Social Security district Office

What is Medi-Medi?

Medi-Medi refers to health insurance only and **does not refer to a cash payment.** Medi-Medi means a person has a confirmed disability (or old age) and has both Medicare and MediCal coverage. MediCal is the secondary insurance; Medicare remains the **primary** insurance.

What are Medicare Advantage Programs?

Medicare Advantage Programs are usually offered by health insurance companies that cover more services with fewer co-pays than Medicare alone. Many of these programs require the insured to sign over their Medicare coverage to the provider. The insured person usually agrees to obtain all medical care through the health network unless the network pre-approves specialty services or there is a 911 emergency services occurrence.

Can I keep my Medicare coverage separate from a group if I have MediCal as my secondary health insurance?

Currently in California that is allowed. Be careful to work with someone who is knowledgeable about your personal situation such as your mental health practitioner.

What if I don't like the plan I've signed up for? May I change?

Ability to change for some plans can be done within 2-6 weeks, depending on the date of your request. Other plans have a specific time of the calendar year called *open enrollment*. Changes may be made only during that time of year and may only become effective after the close of that period. This is similar to many employer plans.

What is a representative payee?

It is not uncommon for the Social Security Administration, based on medical evidence provided during the processing of a claim, to request that the claimant's SSI or SSDI funds be paid to a third party (not to be confused with conservatorship).

What is temporary disability?

If a person has worked and paid into the California state employment fund and becomes unable to work, that person can/should immediately apply for temporary disability (rather than unemployment) through the California State Employment Development Department. No matter how much a claimant has paid in, there is a maximum length of payments allowable. In the past this has been one year to cover the gap between the period of initial onset of disability and the length of time required by the Social Security Administration to be eligible to apply for SSDI/SSI. The value of this program is that it provides the injured employee temporary funding to avoid homelessness. Should the disability become longer term and the injured worker applies for SSDI, on approval a portion of the SSDI is owed back to the State of California. This program is state specific and is not available in all states.

Pitfalls to Watch For

- Unscrupulous people who insert themselves to become payees, including family members who have historically been unwilling to support the claimant.

- Parents who become representative payees should be mindful that the money must be spent on behalf of the claimant with proof of the disbursement of the funds. The Social Security Administration will randomly call representative payees in to show their accounting of the funds. A portion of the claimant's funds can be used for rent, food, transportation, etc.

An adult son does not remember receiving his money from his mother. What should she do? (Domestic Abuse Intervention Project.)

Power & Control

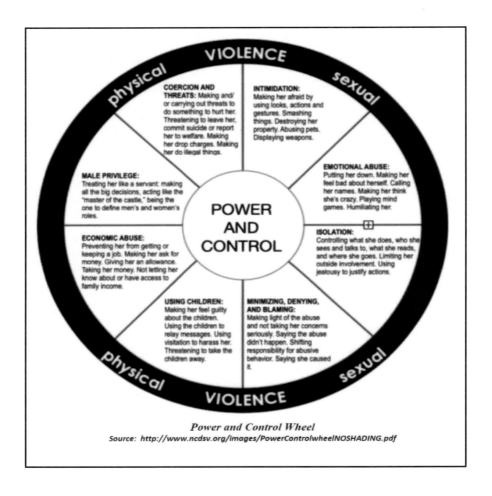

Power and Control Wheel
Source: http://www.ncdsv.org/images/PowerControlwheelNOSHADING.pdf

Since claimants are often assertive about their rights once the funds begin to be paid, it is helpful to maintain a separate bank account for the management of these funds. In the event you are giving the claimant any cash at all, it is helpful to keep a spiral notebook for the claimant to sign and date every time he/she receives cash.

- It often increases tensions between adult siblings when one sibling is named representative payee. For these family situations, as well as for aging parents who are still payee, it is often helpful to have a neutral third-party organization to serve as the representative payee. These services may charge a minimal monthly fee. They should be bonded, insured, and subject to audit. They maintain accurate financial records as well as complete any forms required by the Social Security Administration.

- Professional fiduciaries will often not take these cases since the amount of money is small from their perspective.

Recommendation

Professional Fiduciary Office rendering

The State of California should establish a Trust Office that can, on application, act as representative payee for family members and/or for mental health consumers who have demonstrated a consistent pattern of inability to use their monthly income to provide for their housing needs as the result of their mental illness.

** **Note:** Many funding sources for disabilities exist such as specific labor organizations, military, or private disability plans that employees may enroll in. This manual is not intended to address all types of disability payments. The scope of this manual is restricted to the most commonly asked questions about SSI and SSDI.

Summary

The pathway to assembling financial resources for an adult child with SMI can be arduous and time-consuming. In addition, the person who needs assistance may not be in agreement that they have a mental disability and may refuse to apply.

Mental Health Social Service agencies are often helpful in assisting families in obtaining and retaining benefits. While many disability attorneys process SSD/SSI claims, they usually lack the willingness or time to make home calls to rouse a claimant out of bed, encourage them to get dressed, transport them to the often-dreaded appointment with the disability review physician, and assist them in maintaining a degree of calm during the entire process. Attorneys are highly specialized in presenting cases, but they are not clinicians.

Most Important Reminders:

- The approval process can be slow, slow, and slower.

- Obtaining benefits does not mean that the person can never work.

- Obtaining benefits often opens a door to other benefits.

This is a federal benefit. The approval of SSDI and/or SSI is most often bittersweet since it validates in writing that a person has a disability that currently prevents them from being gainfully employed. It is important, however, to view this approval as the key to opening the door to new ways of thinking, new opportunities, and the possibilities of recreating one's life. The disability payments can serve as a bridge that provides a bit of income and medical insurance. Independence and a meaningful life is possible.

CHAPTER 8
A FUNCTIONING PUBLIC MENTAL HEALTH SYSTEM

To date there are currently no known national standards of care for adults who have SMI. How many states have implemented a well-thought-out plan to provide for this niche group? Due to the expense of providing consistent care and proper medications, few private mental health providers accept people with SMI as new patients. Even with the Mental Health Parity Act, public hearings show continuing vast disparities in the provision and insurance approval of purely medical treatment versus mental health treatment. Despite evidence that early intervention in the treatment of psychosis can vastly improve outcomes, many people lack access. Homelessness continues to increase, often in relation to federal funding for housing vouchers through the US Department of Housing and Urban Development (HUD). Inpatient hospitalizations are rapidly becoming inaccessible rendering jails as the default housing.

Things nearly everyone agrees on:

- Law enforcement personnel are an inappropriate resource for the treatment of SMI. This is not why they became law enforcement officers. Conversely, mental health treatment providers did not train to engage in physical altercations.

The two disciplines can be most effective on emergency calls when they interact. Crisis Intervention Team training is helpful as well.

- A *continuum* of housing and treatment options should be available to meet the needs of this unique group.

- While treatment should be patient-focused, family members should be included since they have significant history and can help improve treatment outcomes.

- Public safety and health must be protected.

- Individual civil rights must be balanced against issues of public safety and health.

- Costs to taxpayers should be considered.

- Stigma affects many facets of public mental health care (e.g. attitudes of homeowners' organizations resistant to mental health housing in their neighborhood).

- Availability of mental health care can be affected by lack of access to transportation systems, distance, or scarcity of trained mental health professionals.

- Our current system(s) is not working.

What We Lost with the Closures of State Hospitals

Few who remember the state hospital systems would advocate for their return. Society, however, lost some services that we have failed to transfer into the community. In California, some of those things are:

- Containment of persons exhibiting symptoms of acute psychosis.

- A system that provided community prevocational training.

- Socialization training.

- Containment and protection of vulnerable adults from predatory societal elements.

- Special units of law enforcement trained and focused on working with people with SMI.

- Trust Office services that could act as representative payee for client funds, even after discharge into community placements. The Trust Office had the capacity to divide the SSI payment into rental payment and client funds for personal use. This service alone prevented homelessness for certain clients who consistently mismanaged their funds. No conservatorship was required.

- Thorough initial assessment that included:

  o Antibacterial showering and shampoo.

  o Clean clothes.

  o Thorough physical examination including EEG and EKG.

  o Psychological testing, psychosocial report including family history, and vocational assessment. All specialty reports were submitted and a case conference was held, including the identified patient, to discuss the results and develop a treatment plan. Often an underlying physical disorder was discovered as the reason for the person's psychiatric symptoms, so the person could be treated and released from a psychiatric setting.

- Linkage with a community-based unit to provide continuous care management to the client and the family on discharge back into the community.

- Treatment units for persons with both SMI and substance-abuse-induced psychosis.

- Treatment units available for persons with SMI and marginal IQ test scores with appropriate treatment to build skill levels.

For a more thorough discussion of some of the positives that mental hospitals provided, review Ralph Slovenko's article: *"The Transinstitutionalization of the Mentally Ill."* (Slovenko, Ralph pp 641-660)

What would any public mental health system need to include to provide for Adults and Older Adults who have SMI?

Must-Haves

- Public safety.

- Access to appropriate mental health treatment to include a proper assessment (physical, psychological testing, psychosocial assessment, vocational assessment, etc.).

- Ability to engage with the identified patient, even when he/she does not agree he/she requires services. There should be clear evidence that the refusal is the result of mental illness and evidence-based data that indicate medical intervention would be highly likely to reduce the symptoms interfering with ability to function in major areas of life.

- Sufficient legal structure to require treatment for 90 days. Identified patients would not be required to remain on an inpatient status during that period, but the 90-day hold could require them to remain in recommended treatment modalities similar to the 12-step model that often recommends "90 meetings in 90 days."

- Housing options that provide a continuum of models based on the needs of the client. These may range from models with built-in permanent supportive services such as adult residential care facilities (which can provide a temporary bridge from acute psychosis to independent living) to transitional housing, independent housing, peer-run shared housing, ranch housing with active participation by residents in such activities as gardening and tending animals, and shared two-bedroom housing to name a few options.

Licensed Board and Care home (Smith, LA Times)

- Protective services for the residents from predators is essential in all models. Residents must be guaranteed safety.

Access to prevocational resources is needed

- Access to prevocational resources and/other resources so the identified patient can self-evaluate his/her abilities to sustain part-time interest groups or return to work without penalty.

- Families and identified patients benefit from a team-based continuity-of-care approach that has the capacity to follow clients and their families long term.

- The current system requires clients constantly to re-engage with each community and hospital provider as well as to deal with the multiple reassignments of clinical staff members within the same organization. There needs to be a **single-point-of-entry team** that knows the family and the identified patient and remains as a point of reference throughout the course of treatment.

- Mental health courts and diversion options.

- Jails, the treatment of last resort, are ill-equipped to help adults who have SMI. At best people are contained.

  o Research done by the Los Angeles County District Attorney (2015) showed that the capacity of a person with SMI to learn consequences and not reoffend was low. Jails for SMI are not an effective tool..

  o The cost to taxpayers is significantly higher than if mental health treatment was provided in a mental health environment. Because law enforcement is classified as a high-risk job, the pay and retirement benefits of law enforcement personnel are vastly different than those of a mental health provider seeing the same person. Compounding those costs are the costs associated with the legal process such as transportation to and from jail and the court-room [judge, clerk, bailiff, attorneys, etc.] (Perry, Laist.com)

- o Mental health courts and diversion strategies are being tried in areas such as Los Angeles County. Curiously, the staff members involved are not part of the Department of Mental Health. Currently there seems to be a lack of coordination between the Office of Diversion and Reentry (ODR) program, under the Department of Health Services, and the Department of Mental Health.

- A system to reintegrate people from prisons who have a substantiated history of mental health issues as well as physical and/or previous addiction health issues.

- An open-door policy that offers identified patients reassurance that when they've met their goals and want to terminate treatment, they can always return. Often identified patients will choose to return to previous patterns as they try to process what is/is not a part of having mental illness.

- A Trust Office to act as representative payee.

- Protective services need to be provided by persons who have mental health clinical training to intercede on behalf of identified patients and/or family members who are at risk or currently being abused. **All complaints should be referred to law enforcement agencies for investigation regardless of whether the abused person is willing to sign a complaint,** has family income above the federal poverty guidelines, or any other reason. People deserve to be safe from predatory, abusive, or intimidating behaviors from others. This should include adults who have SMI and their families.

Nice to Have:

- Interagency collaboration to facilitate coordination of care between the agencies engaged with various aspects of providing services to the same person.

- Long-term housing options providing the following: medication support, prevocational and/or vocational opportunities, and a behavioral incentive program to move from shared occupancy to single occupancy to transitional living, then on to independent living while retaining access to the original support structure.

- A rate of reimbursement to ARFs and RCFEs specific to adults who have SMI with complex needs. (Wisner)

- Services to meet the needs of specialty demographics including but not limited to:

- o Adults with both SMI and substance abuse.

- o Adults with both SMI and IQs between 71 and 99.

- Services that provide early psychosis treatment.

- Federal tax dollars to fund mental health services.

- Recognition of the role that the federal budget sequestration has continued to play in the rise of homelessness with the loss of funding for housing subsidies for people who have low-incomes such as SSI/SSDI (National Priorities)

"How the Sausage Gets Made"

A fundamental problem in creating public mental health services lies in the very nature of legislation. *The process appears to be something like this:*

- A problem is noticed in the community.

- The problem, likely not a new one, grows, and grows, and grows like Jack's beanstalk.

- When Jack's beanstalk begins to negatively impact a lot of voters, politicians decide to address the problem, but then argue about how. This is partic-ularly true if the problem cannot be monetized into profit for the private sector.

- Legislation is finally created. Proposed regulations are presented to members of the community currently called stakeholders.

- The new bill is finally implemented.

Inherent in this process are underlying problems rarely addressed. There is always a group of folks who opposed having the legislation passed at all, so they work to undermine the effectiveness of the bill, leaving loopholes for them to revisit the bill later in ways that benefit them.

Due to the nature of our democracy with its rotation of leadership, there are always new legislators with new staff who may/may not be acquainted with the history of this issue. Their task is to focus on the present and how best to represent the interests of their constituencies. Thus, there is not a blending of the best practices of the past being brought forward to create a new bill that incorporates forward thinking built on a foundation from the past.

Case Example: Why It Matters

The public mental health system in the state of California had many parts that worked well in the community such as:

- Community psychiatric social services programs.

- A network of statewide offices that could accommodate clients who wished to relocate but needed supportive services immediately.

- Ability to link with incarcerated clients prior to their release and to make arrangements for housing, medications, etc.

- Clinical staff to assess a client prior to calling for emergency psychiatric services.

- Clinical staff to ride along with law enforcement officers on potential 5150 calls.

- Tiered reimbursement system for adult residential facilities.

These and other services were gradually discontinued **due to lack of funding** for the mental health system in the period between approximately 1980 and 2010.

When the Mental Health Services Act passed, the problem had become big enough for the voters to pass a special tax to "fix mental health." Great! Exciting! A life raft for mental health. Notice, however, that as wonderful as it is (and it is wonderful), it specifically excludes funding for the normal administration and ongoing functions of mental health departments. California's state mental health system, and many of its county mental health offices, experienced **annual reductions in their funding** for over 20 years.

Imagine your home had no maintenance for over 20 years. No pest control, no painting the patio cover, no new wallpaper, no plumbing repairs, etc. because your budget was reduced each and every year. You weren't free to go out and get money elsewhere because there were rules about that.

Along the way people pass your home, which eventually begins to look pretty shabby. Passersby judge your home as substandard. They also judge you, the homeowner, as a person who doesn't know how to take proper care of their home. Eventually someone comes along and gives you money but tells you not to spend any of it on past due repairs, just buy new stuff you don't currently have. That money looks enticing so you take it. You go out and purchase the things you're allowed to. But what about those past due repairs that you still don't have the money to address? They're still there.

Then along comes another problem (homelessness among folks with mental illness) and again the process repeats. Legislation is created to solve that specific problem with never an awareness of the structures that had previously existed (and still exist) that are/were very effective, very cost -effective, but forgotten. Keep in mind, licensed ARFs are a prime example of an effective program that is languishing and barely treading water.

If it were not for those facilities, the homeless population would be exponentially worse. It is extremely disrespectful to all of those folks who have sacrificed personally to continue to provide services to adults with SMI, and are now excluded when new funding comes available. This is particularly true when one compares the funding for temporary housing, such as shelter beds, to the funding that licensed permanent housing that specializes in providing care and supervision receives.

Summary

One of the reasons our government works/does not work is because there are always competing interests whose voices may/may not be heard. Public mental health, therefore, is always created by publicly elected officials who represent their constituencies. That is their job. Keep in mind that elected officials are not mental health clinicians. Additionally, elected officials, by definition, are temporarily in that position, especially with the advent of more term limits. Laws are often created with minimal information, lack of time, and the need to please many perspectives. Often people who have the most information regarding a particular issue are paid lobbyists. Where are the lobbyists for adults with SMI and their families?

Remember this when evaluating our public mental health systems. If we want better policies there is a need for greater input from the personnel already implementing current policies, the families, end users, and other stakeholders of the public mental health system. Clearly our public mental health systems across the nation are failing to meet the needs of society, families, staff, and most of all Adults who have SMI.

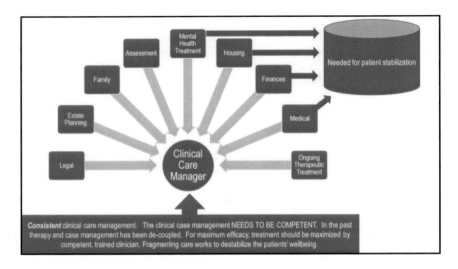

Clinical Care Model

CHAPTER 9:
WHAT WORKS FOR BARBARA WILSON: A MODEL OF CARE

Barbara's Clinical Care model

If you had a widget or a medication that worked nearly 90% of the time, how fast would you want to use it? If there was a methodology of providing services to adults with SMI even 60% of the time, would you be interested or even impressed? I have been using a method for many years that is consistently effective. When compared to the costs of not treating people with SMI, it's also a cost savings, especially to taxpayers. How do we do this magic? What's the secret sauce? Here it is! *Consistency.* We provide services to adults who have SMI and their families.

A consistent clinical care management team provides continuity of care. Therapy and case management are coupled. Barbara Wilson's "magic method" has provided consistently effective services to adults who have SMI and their families. These are some basic steps.

Assess and Create a Plan

I meet with the client and the entire family. Everyone has an opportunity to speak their truth and to be heard. Based on that meeting, together we arrive at a plan that addresses their immediate and future needs. We take into account their value system, including religious tenets, ethnicity, the desired location if placement is an issue, and their financial status.

Implement the Plan

In order to implement the plan, the family, identified client, and I divide up various roles. Because transportation can often be a barrier to access, we may provide the transportation to ensure that the person gets to whatever service is needed and/or we will meet the client there. **We never send the identified clients into appointments without a team member.** We know many unexpected issues can suddenly arise that might defeat the very purpose for which we're there. This is less about enabling and more about guaranteeing a successful outcome. Applying to large systems for benefits would be overwhelming to a person without SMI. It is only prudent to accompany our clients and stay with them throughout their processes.

Even if there is no identifiable family, we still engage with the client and support the client in every single appointment we make. Every appointment? Yes, every appointment! It is time well spent because it often facilitates for the client, who is often overwhelmed and experiencing high levels of anxiety. Moreover, it provides a casual environment in which to build rapport.

By the time clients get to me, they have usually been to many other providers, clinics, psychiatrists, and psychologists, not to mention other case managers. Yet, their lives are still not working. We understand that frustration. We also understand when clients share, "just thinking about going to see a clinician in an office raises my anxiety." Because the identified client, however symptomatic, is a part of the original planning, they are usually cooperative. There are exceptions however. One example is resistance to applying for disability benefits because the person does not agree he/she has mental illness. Still, over time, I am usually successful in obtaining cooperation.

Enrollment in community support services such as adult day programs, intensive outpatient programs, and 12-step programs is very important. Mental illness is a disease of **isolation**. Participation in community-based programs helps people move from isolation and hopelessness to a sense of hope and the possibility of resuming a life after an acute episode. I strongly believe in helping clients build a "tool chest with portable tools." That is, introducing clients (and their families) to resources they can use and control access/use without my continued oversight.

Given the limited funding and available resources for growth and independence, a person with lived experience might need to be willing to relocate to an adult residential facility. This can be a very difficult decision for both the client and the family.

Much like going away to college, having some physical distance allows both the family members and the identified patient to readjust their relationship. For many families it allows them to become family members again instead of being utilized as a case manager or "medication patrol."

When the identified client begins to have his/her own separate treatment team, my role recedes. I remain involved with the team, their staff, the identified client, and the family for periodic case conferences. If funding is an issue, I facilitate the disability applications and represent claimants in a hearing if needed. I also maintain relationships with disability attorneys I respect. I only represent claimants with SMI because often their mental illness interferes with their ability to open their mail or show up for appointments at a specified time. This process can be hugely time-consuming. Few attorneys have the willingness or the resources to focus the amount of time required.

Over time the identified client may or may not relapse as happens with any chronic illness. The difference in having continuity of care is that when relapse occurs, neither the client nor the family has to revisit their entire history with a new person. We simply pick up where we left off. I may even facilitate the hospitalization since a part of my work is to encourage the identified client to recognize their own symptoms prior to the onset of an episode. In that way, they can begin to take charge of their mental illness and their recovery with support.

Ongoing Support for the Family

This is a key ingredient in helping the family regain a level of peace and serenity as well as helping them restore appropriate boundaries with their adult child.

It's a simple plan that works almost every single time. So why aren't we doing it? *Insurance doesn't cover it because it's too time-consuming.* It utilizes too many units of service. (Units of service is a time measurement that many health insurers require.) Government-funded services may or may not cover it. *That depends on current levels of taxpayer dollars and political will.*

Which costs taxpayers more? Adults with SMI who are homeless or adults who get our model of treatment? An adult with SMI who has no treatment and is in front of your business or an adult with SMI treated by a professionally trained mental health team?

Does the lack of community-based programs for adults who have SMI impact your business? Your neighborhood? Your community library where you take your children? Your local grocery stores? Your use of public beaches? The choice is yours. The results are too.

Case Example: How it Works (fictitious names, fictitious case)

John Doe was referred for services by his mother, Katherine. Both Katherine and her husband, Bryan, had tried for more than 20 years to find a solution to John's problems.

John's first psychotic episode began when he was away at college. At that time John and his parents assumed whatever happened was a one-time event. Katherine wondered aloud about one of his dorm residents having slipped something into his soda. Perhaps this was the reason why he needed psychiatric hospitalization. Something in his soda had made him act crazy.

After some discussion, the parents agreed to leave John in school and returned home. The unplanned trip presented a hiccup in their budget, but it was a medical necessity. They had good insurance, thank goodness, and so the costs were manageable. John was 19 at the time.

John's View

At 43 years old, John is now bedraggled and homeless. He is an embarrassment to himself and to his family. While he had finished college in the top 10% of his class, he struggled with social relationships. He often missed social cues and nuances. While he once expected to achieve a high-status position in his field, and perhaps even out earn his father's upper-middle-class status, he has been unable to maintain sustained employment.

In his 30s he was in and out of hospitals, clinics, and outpatient programs. Depression set in as he realized he was unlikely to achieve his dreams. News of neighborhood friends getting married, having children, and buying a home served only to reinforce his gnawing sense that he was never going to be successful. Even his younger siblings were successfully employed and doing well. What was wrong with him? He was smart, ambitious, and didn't smoke or drink. And sex? Well, he had strict morals, no sex before marriage. And he believed he shouldn't get married unless he had a job and could support a family.

Why can't I do anything right?

Katherine's View

At the time Katherine called me for help, John was homeless. In his last apartment, he became convinced there was a camera inside the ceiling light fixture in his bedroom. He dismantled the entire mechanism so that he could sleep without being spied on. He had stopped paying rent and refused to leave his small apartment by barricading himself with a deadbolt lock he'd installed. The landlord called the police. On interviewing John, they wrote a 5150 hold and once again he was hospitalized involuntarily. Following the hospitalization John went missing. Katherine couldn't find him.

Katherine had two issues: the fear that gripped her on not knowing the whereabouts of her son, and concern for providing for his needs once she and her husband died. Who would answer his daily phone calls in which he often rambled? John often called 16 times within an hour, from early morning until past midnight. Katherine and Bryan had taken him to all the best psychiatrists and psychologists. He would get better for a period of time. Eventually he would stop taking his medications and go downhill.

Katherine had additional worries. She was nearing retirement. Bryan had already retired. He had a number of health issues. She needed to be more engaged with supporting Bryan, taking him to his medical appointments, picking up his medications and making certain they never ran out, organizing his pills, making special meals the doctor ordered but that he didn't like to eat. The list was endless and she was exhausted.

What Works for Barbara Wilson

I held a family meeting with Katherine, Bryan, the siblings, and the grandparents via teleconference. Normally John would've been included but he was homeless at that time and was not responding to phone calls. Everybody was able to share their concerns and desired outcomes.

This was the first time the entire family actually came together and openly spoke about John's mental illness. Katherine had always assumed someone in the family would pick up where she left off after her death. She hadn't realized the depth of intense rage and sense of neglect her other children felt toward her and Bryan. Katherine was visibly shaken. The number one request to me from the siblings: help our parents, especially Mom, develop some boundaries with John.

Outreach and Engagement

I began by leaving messages on John's cell phone to introduce myself. I asked for a call back.

Over time we agreed to meet at various coffee shops where he didn't show. I didn't give up.

Following a 2.5-hour wait at a Denny's restaurant, I was about to leave when he showed up. He was carrying all of his belongings in a trash bag.

Meeting the Immediate Need

Following a meal, John agreed to ride with me to safe housing that I had negotiated for him in case he was willing. There he could have a consistent place to sleep. He could share a room with only one other person. He had access to a bathroom, food, and safety. He agreed to consider taking his medications.

Busy, Busy, Busy

Over the next 3–6 months our team members transported John to various social service agencies to obtain funding, medical coverage, and mental health resources. Because these agencies tend to be very large organizations, we explained what we were about to do: that there are a lot of people in the building, security personnel may be present and require us all to be checked, what questions they're likely to ask, etc. We also developed signals we agreed John could use to inform us if he needed to take a break.

We participated in the encounters with the staff members of each agency. We got copies of any paperwork given to John. We made backup copies of everything to store in his files. We were his back-up computer for now. Our goal was to reduce his stress. After each agency encounter, we went out to eat. John got to choose from two or three affordable options. My treat. We debriefed. When we took John back to the residence, especially if it was an adult residential facility, we always entered the facility with John, explained to the staff what we'd done and handed off any paperwork for John's records while retaining copies for our records.

John and the Legal System

If court appearances were required, we transported John to ensure he was there on time but also so he had support from his team. We were usually successful in negotiating agreements that both protected society and protected John's interests. Over time, even if John had to be re-hospitalized, because of the consistency of our team's involvement, there would be less trauma associated with the event. Moreover, his residence wouldn't have changed so there would be consistency and predictability.

This initial period of righting the ship can easily take 1–2 years and can often require 40 hours per month. Costly? Perhaps. On the other hand, what is the cost to taxpayers of using our current disjointed system of care with constant turnover and lack of continuity?

Don't Overlook the Family

I regard the family as part of the case rather than John Doe, Individual. Why?

- Katherine's trauma of living through the many episodes of her son's illness has often gone unaddressed and certainly untreated. I listen to Katherine as she shares her history of John's illness. I also gently probe her to gauge her levels of self-care, anxiety, grief, fears, physical illnesses, and support network. I urge her to notice her own needs. I explore medical and community resources that can help her address her needs.

- Both parents need to address end-of-life planning for John's share of their estate so that they relieve their other adult children of that burden. It can't be stated often enough that most adult children who have SMI do not want their siblings in charge of their financial lives. Conversely, many adult siblings, if allowed to be honest, do not want the respon-sibility. Nonprofit organizations or fiduciaries can perform this function. We freely make referrals. We have no financial connection with any referrals we make.

- Our team acts as a sounding board to the family, especially Katherine, as she continues to have concerns about how to engage/set boundaries with John.

- Once we've gotten John into a community mental health program, we request periodic conferences with their staff members, him, and his parents. The goal is to maintain integrated care. We also know nearly all programs are time-limited. That's why we want to remain engaged. As John leaves one program, we're there to ensure he doesn't fall between the cracks going forward.

- Periodically we create special rituals to honor the growth and progress John has made, often with his family and friends in attendance.

Maintenance

While there are always peaks and valleys, the use of emergency services goes down as John and his family begin to trust there is always a back-up team available to them. During this phase, contact with John is significantly decreased because his daily schedule is full with activities that he has scheduled for himself. He has a routine with significant support.

A word of caution: Often during this phase when everything is going smoothly, a client will discontinue taking medications and eventually relapse. While this can be a very painful experience for those who have worked with him/her, it is entirely natural for a person with a disability to wonder what he/she can accomplish without the training wheels. I view this as the person running their own experiment once again. Just be patient and, above all, be consistent. Be present if they're open to it. And most of all, your gift to all the Johns is that they don't have to begin from the beginning. They know that you know their story. John Doe just has to bring you up to date since the last time you talked when he's ready to re-engage. You're both in it for the long haul!

Summary: The Arc of Treatment and Recovery from Serious Mental Illness

There is an arc of treatment and recovery from SMI. This includes:

- Engagement.

- Active implementation of the treatment plan with continual adjustments along the way.

- Stabilizing mental health symptoms (this may even require a brief rehospitalization).

- Longer periods of stability with shorter periods of acute distress.

- Both the client and the family begin to agree that there is SMI sufficient that it interferes with the client's ability to maintain sustained employment, school, military service, or other activities that require sustained concentration and orderly thinking.

- Both the client and the family begin to accept that the patient is capable of building a life with purpose, although it may not be the life either one planned.

- Both the client and the family begin to accept the need for sustained supportive services, especially from consistent personnel with whom there is a trust relationship.

As Oprah says, "What I Know for Sure..."

- Adults with SMI did not grow up with a goal of having a mental illness that interfered with their ability to function.

- When adults with SMI are offered quality mental health services with consistency, compassion, and patience they can and do get better.

- Verbal therapy is often denied to adults with SMI because their insurance will not provide coverage. I **believe this is a serious mistake.**

- Adults with SMI are often the canaries in the coal mine. We have treated them as disposable persons not worthy of having opportunities to achieve. If we have one group of human beings who we as a society regard as throwaways, how much easier will it become to view other whole groups as throwaways as well?

- Most parents would rather have their adult children have access to treatment, even if their civil rights are violated, than to have them die with their civil rights intact. That is not about control. That is about wanting to keep their child alive.

- Adults who have SMI need help in processing their self-hatred and shame at having a mental illness.

- Adults who have SMI have lower life expectancies than do their counterparts who do not.

- Adults with SMI need vocational opportunities and prevocational opportunities that can accommodate time off when they relapse.

- Not all people who are homeless have SMI, although the trauma of being homeless can contribute to mental illness.

- Not all people who have SMI are homeless. It is a mistake to conflate them. That said, if a person is receiving SSI, where exactly does he/she live if receiving a monthly income of less than $1,000 in California?

- Adults with SMI may be very intelligent and have many talents. It is insulting to say "They're not crazy all the time," "He's so intelligent too," "Do you think there's a thin line between smart and crazy?" These offhand remarks reflect ignorance of the disordered thinking SMI creates.

- We must work diligently to help identified clients and families avoid burnout.

GLOSSARY AND COMMON
HEALTH TERMS

AOT	Assisted Outpatient Treatment
ARF	State Licensed Adult Residential Facility aka "Board & Care"
Bi-Polar Disorder	Brain Disease – Newer Terminology
CBT	Cognitive Behavioral Therapy
CCL	Community Care Licensing – State Agency that licenses Adult Residential Facilities
Co-Occurring	Persons having more than one diagnosis
CSS	Community Services & Supports
DCFS	Department of Children and Family Services
DHS	Department of Health Services
Directly Operated Mental Health Services	Services from agencies that are a part of the Department of Mental Health vs Contracted Services (mental health services provided by agencies who have contracted with Department of Mental Health).
DMH	Department of Mental Health
DPH	Department of Public Health
DPSS	Department of Public Social Services
DSM-5	Diagnostic Statistical Manual of Mental Disorders Current Fifth Edition
DV	Domestic Violence
EDPNA	Eligible for Direct Pay non-Attorney
EVP	Evidence Based Practices (vs. "Promising Practices")
FCCS	Field Capable Clinical Services (Home Visits)

Fiscal Year	July 1–June 30 for both state and county; October 1-September 30 for federal
FSP	Full-Service Partnership
GR	General Relief
HIPAA	Health Insurance Portability and Accountability Act
HOME	Homeless Outreach and Mobile Engagement
IMD	Institution for Mental Diseases (aka locked or secure facility). (See IMD exclusion.)
Independent Living Home	Community based residential housing, usually not state-licensed
IS	Integrated System
LCSW	Licensed Clinical Social Worker
LPS Act-California Hospital Association	The LPS Act refers to Sections 5150, 5151 and 5152 of the Welfare and Institutions Code. It is a California law governing the involuntary civil commitment of individuals that due to mental illness pose a danger to self, a danger to others, or who are gravely disabled and require inpatient psychiatric care.
LPS 5150	Lanterman Petris Short Act defining the criteria for Involuntary Mental Health Confinement and Treatment (California)
MAT	Medication-Assisted Therapy
Medicaid	Aka MediCal in California
Medi-Medi	Health Coverage: Medicare + MediCal
MET Team	Mental Evaluation Team
MHCLP	Mental Health Court Linkage Program
MHFA	Mental Health First Aid
MHSA	Mental Health Services Act

MORS	Milestones of Recovery Scale
OA	Older Adult (60+)
ODR	Office of Diversion and Reentry
PG	Office of Public Guardian
PMRT	Psychiatric Mobile Response Team (aka PET Team)
PRRCH	Peer-Run Respite Care Homes
RCFE	Residential Care Facility for Elderly
Rep Payee	Representative payee—person who receives payments on behalf of another
SSA	Social Security Administration
SNF	Skilled Nursing Facility
Sober Living Facility	Residential facility, generally not licensed
SPMI or SMI	Severe and Persistently Adults with Serious Mental Illness or Serious Mental Illness
SRO	Single-Room Occupancy (a type of housing, often subsidized)
SSI	Supplemental Security Income
Stigma	Belief that people with mental illness should be silent, shuttered away from society, erased
TAY	Transitional-Age Youth (ages 16–24)
Transitional Facility	Community-based facility that can permit residents to regain life skills such as meal preparations, housekeeping chores, etc.
UCC	Urgent Care Center(s)

CITATIONS

1. "Social Darwinism." Encyclopedia Britannica. www.britannica.com/topic/social-Darwinism.

2. Live testimony from a survivor of a lobotomy is shared in the following article: www.npr.org/2005/11/16/5014080/my-lobotomy-howard-dullys-journey.

3. Roth, D., Bean, J., Stefl, M. E., & Howe, S.R. 1985. *Homelessness in Ohio: Findings from a Statewide Study. Ohio Department of Mental Health, Office of Program Evaluation and Research.* www.ncbi.nlm.nih.gov/books/NBK218236.

4. https://da.lacounty.gove/sites/default/files/policies/Mental-health-Report-072915.pdf.

5. Torrey, E. F. (2014). American Psychosis: How the Federal Government Destroyed the Mental Illness Treatment System. New York: Oxford University Press.

6. Abramson, M. (1972). The criminalization of mentally disordered behavior. *Journal of Hospital & Community Psychiatry, 23*(4), 101-105.

7. Information and Technical Assistance on the American Disabilities Act, ADA.gov

8. Abramson, ibid

9. Samson, C. (1990). Inequality, the New Right and mental health care delivery in the United States in the Reagan era. Critical Social Policy, 10(29), 40–57. https://doi.org/10.1177/026101839001002903

10. Lacey, J. (2015). *Mental Health Advisory Board Report*. https://da.lacounty.gov/sites/default/files/policies/Mental-Health-Report-072915.pdf.

11. Holliday, Stephanie Brooks, Nicholas M. Pace, Neil Gowensmith, Ira Packer, Daniel Murrie, Alicia Virani, Bing Han, and Sarah B. Hunter, *Estimating the Size of the Los Angeles County Jail Mental Health Population Appropriate for Release into Community Services*, Santa Monica, Calif.: RAND Corporation, RR-4328-LAC, 2020. As of May 22, 2022: https://www.rand.org/pubs/research_reports/RR4328.html.

12. Placzek, J. (n.d.) *Did the Emptying of Mental Hospitals Contribute to Homelessness?* www.kqed.org/news/11209729/did-the-emptying-of-mental-hospitals-contribute-to-homelessness-here.

13. https://leginfo.legislature.ca.gov/faces/billTextClient.xhtml?bill_id=201920200SB803

14. Mechanic, D. & Olfson, M. (2016). The relevance of the Affordable Care Act for improving mental health care," *Annual Review of Clinical Psychology, 12*, 515–542. Disabilityjustice.org/olmstead-v-lc

15. Barry, L., & Huskamo, H. A..(2011, September 15). Moving beyond parity—Mental health and addiction care under the ACA. *New England Journal of Medicine*, 973-975.

16. www.commonwealthfund.org/blog/2020/aca-10-how-has-it-impacted-mental-health-care.

17. https://calmatters.org/health/2021/09/988-911-funding-crisis-hotline-suicide-california/

18. LPS Act—California Hospital Association. www.calhospital.org/lps-act.

19. https://namila.org/resources/guide-to-lps-conservatorship-family/

20. Center on Juveniles and Criminal Justice, cjcj.org

21. California Association of Local Behavioral Health Board and Commissions. https://www.calbhbc.org/lauras-law.html

22. Symon, Evan. (2020.) Several Mental Health Reforming Bills Signed by Gov.Newsom. https://www.theunion.com/news/gov-gavin-newsom-oks-expansion-of-lauras-law-throughout-california/https://californiaglobe.com/section-2/several-mental-health-reforming-bills-signed-by-gov-newsom/.

23. Tsai, G., & Quanbeck, C. GARY TSAI, M.D. & CAMERON QUANBECK, M.D. *Assisted Outpatient*

Treatment- Proactive Care for the Severely Mentally Ill "Laura's Law". As of May 29, 2022: https://slide-player.com/slide/4723576/

24. George,Karen & Ma, Patrick, *Serving Children, Youth and their Families with Mental Health Services in New and Innovative Ways Karen George Patrick Ma.* As of May 29, 2022: https://slideplayer.com/slide/9233065/, 2022 May 29

25. https://namila.org/resources/guide-to-lps-conservatorship-family/

26. Wisner, J. (2021, Oct.) *No Time to Waste: An Imminent Housing Crisis for People with Serious Mental Illness Living in Adult Residential Facilities.* https://www.chhs.ca.gov/wp-content/uploads/2021/11/Housing-That-Heals-11-05-21.pdf

27. https://time.com/6075859/britney-spears-conservatorship-disability/

28. https://calmatters.org/health/2021/09/988-911-funding-crisis-hotline-suicide-california/

29. Wisner, ibid

30. Kubler-Ross, E. (1969). *On Death and Dying.* New York: Macmillan Publishing.

31. Closing Psychiatric Hospitals Seemed Humane, but the State Failed to Build a System to Replace Them." https://apps.bostonglobe.com/

spotlight/the-desperate-and-the-dead/series/
families/?p1=Spotlight_MI_Overview_Read

32. Sherin, J. & Stern, H. (2020, December 18).
"Op-Ed: Our Mental Health Laws are Failing."
www.latimes.com/opinion/story/2020-12-18/
need-for-new-laws-to-address-homelessness

33. State Mental Hospitals Closed to Give People
with Mental Illness Greater Freedom." (2016).
https://apps.bostonglobe.com/spotlight/
the-desperate-and-the-dead/series/community-care/

34. Sherin, & Stern, ibid

35. https//www.providencejournal.com/story/
lifestyle/2014/09/19/catholic-churchs-an-
nulment-criteria-when-deciding-wheth-
er-to-grant-declaration-of-nullity/983983007

36. "Power and Control Wheel." Domestic Abuse
Intervention Project. http://www.ncdsv.org/images/
PowerControlwheelNOSHADING.pdf

37. Slovenko, R. (2003). Transinstitutionalization of the
mentally ill. *Ohio Northern University Law Review,
29*, 641-660.

38. Smith, Doug. "These Homes Keep
LA's Most Vulnerable From Becoming
Homeless. Now They're Closing." www.

latimes.com/california/story/2019-11-06/
homeless-housing-board-care-homes-mental-illnes.

39. Wisner, ibid

40. https://www.nationalpriorities.org/blog/2012/05/02/
pie-week-discretionary-budget/

BIBLIOGRAPHY

Adult Residential Facilities. (2018, March). *Report*. https://www.dhcs.ca.gov/services/MH/Documents/Legislation-Committee/2018-ARF-Final.pdf

Auerback, A. (1959). The Short-Doyle Act; California community mental health services program: Background and status after one year. *California Medicine*, 90(5), 335-338.

Bachrach, L. L. (1993). Continuity of care and approaches to case management for long-term mentally ill patients. *Hospital and Community Psychiatry, 44*(5), 465-468.

Bathen, S. (2020, Aug. 6). *Auditor slams state mental health system, revives Lauras Law*. https://capitolweekly.net/auditor-slams-state-mental-health-system-revives-lauras-law/

Bathen, S. (2020, Sept 3). Lawmakers send historic mental health bills to Newsom. https://steinberginstitute.org/lawmakers-send-historic-mental-health-bills-to-newsom-2/

Baumgartner, J. C., Aboulafia, G. N., & McIntosh, A. (2020, April 3). *The ACA at 10: How has it impacted mental health care?* www.commonwealthfund.org/blog/2020/aca-10-how-has-it-impacted-mental-health-care

Boston Globe (2016, June 23). The desperate and the dead: Families in fear. https://bostonglobe.com/spotlight/the-desperate-and-the-dead/series/families/

Catney, R. (2020). *A Laboratory of Social Policy: California, the New Right and the Gubernatorial Administration of Ronald Reagan, 1967-1975* (Masters thesis, Queen's University, Kingston, Ontario). https://qspace.library.queensu.ca/handle/1974/27888

Chesler, P. (1972). *Women and Madness*. Ann Arbor, MI: University of Michigan.

Day, E. (2008, Jan. 13). *He was so bad, they put an ice pick in his brain.* https://www.theguardian.com/science/2008/jan/13/neuroscience.medicalscience

Disability Rights California (2018, Jan 8). *Understanding the Landerman-Petris-Short Act.* www.disabilityrightsca.org/publications/understanding-the-lanterman-petris-short-lps-act

Domestic Abuse Intervention Project (n.d.) Power and Control Wheel. http://www.ncdsv.org/images/PowerControlwheelNOSHADING.pdf

Drake, R. E., Skinner, J. S., Bond, G. R., & Goldman, H. H. (2009). Social Security and mental illness: Reducing disability with supported employment. *Health Affairs (Millwood)*, 28(3), 761-770.

Ensuring access to quality behavioral health care in our country. (nd). www.paritytrack.org

GARY TSAI, M.D. & CAMERON QUANBECK, M.D. *Assisted Outpatient Treatment - Proactive Care for the Severely*

Mentally Ill "Laura's Law". As of May 29, 2022: https://slide-player.com/slide/4723576/,

Hershbin, L. D. (2009). Gender, age, and diagnosis: The rise and fall of involution melancholia in American psychiatry, 1900–1980." *Bulletin of Historical Medicine, 83*, 710–745.

Holliday, Stephanie Brooks, Nicholas M. Pace, Neil Gowensmith, Ira Packer, Daniel Murrie, Alicia Virani, Bing Han, and Sarah B. Hunter, *Estimating the Size of the Los Angeles County Jail Mental Health Population Appropriate for Release into Community Services*, Santa Monica, Calif.: RAND Corporation, RR-4328-LAC, 2020. As of May 22, 2022: https://www.rand.org/pubs/research_reports/RR4328.html

Information and Technical Assistance on the American Disabilities Act. (nd). https://www.ada.gov/ta-pubs-pg2.htm)

Institute of Medicine (US) Committee on health care for home-less people (1988). Homelessness, health, and human needs. New York: National Academies Press. www.ncbi.nlm.nih.gov/books/NBK218236/

Jacobs, C., Galton, E., & Howard, B. (1999, Feb.) *A New Vision for Mental Health Treatment Laws* (Report). https://menta-lillnesspolicy.org/wp-content/uploads/lps-reform.pdf

Keyes, C. L. M. (2002). The Mental Health Continuum: From languishing to flourishing in life. *Journal of Health and Social Behavior, 43*, 207-222.

Lamb, H. R., & Backrach, L. L. (2001). Some perspectives on deinstitutionalization. Psychiatric Services, 52(3), 1039-1045.

Mechanic, D., & Olfson, M. (2016). The relevance of the Affordable Care Act for improving mental health care," *Annual Review of Clinical Psychology, 12,* 515–542. DisabilityJustice.org/olmstead-v-lc

Mental Health Advisory Board. (2015, August 4). *Report: A blueprint for change.* https://da.lacounty.gov/sites/default/files/policies/Mental-Health-Report-072915.pdf

Mental Health First Aid Organization, https://www.mentalhealthfirstaid.org

Morrison, K. H. (2021, Oct. 26). *For every bed lost, a person is displaced: California's continuing board & care crisis.* https://www.accoglienza.us/for-every-bed-lost-a-person-is-displaced-californias-continuing-board-care-crisis/

Murse, T. (2019, March). *Sequestration and the federal budget.* https://www.thoughtco.com/the-definition-of-sequester-3368278.

National Alliance for the Mentally Ill. www.nami.org

Nolasco, L. (2012). *A policy analysis of the Landerman-Petris-Short Act* (Dissertation, California State-Long Beach). https://www.proquest.com/openview/67b4812b219e1e95337661348d164422/1?pq-origsite=gscholar&cbl=18750&diss=y

Office of Inspector General. (2012). *Review of Short/Doyle Medicaid Payment Rates.* Department of Health and Human Services, A-09-91-00076. Washington DC: BiblioGov.

Perry, N. J. (2020, Jan 7). *More than half of LA County inmates who are mentally ill don't need to be in jail, study finds.* https://laist.com/2020/01/07/mentally-health-jail-la-diversion.php

Powers, R. (2017). *No one cares about crazy people: The chaos and heartbreak of mental health in America.* New York: Hachette Books, 2017.

Putnam, J. K. (2006). Governor Reagan: A reappraisal. *California History*, 84(4).

Reflecting on JFK's legacy of community-based care. (nd). https://www.samhsa.gov/homelessness-programs-resources/hpr-resources/jfks-legacy-community-based-care

Rosenfield, S., Kato, K., & Smith, D. (2017). Gender and mental health. In T. L. Scheid & E. R. Wright, *A handbook for the study of mental health, 3rd ed,* (pp 266-280). Cambridge: Cambridge University Press.

Roth, D., Bean, J., Stefl, M. E., & Howe, S. R. (1985). *Homelessness in Ohio: Findings from a Statewide Study.* Ohio Department of Mental Health, Office of Program Evaluation and Research. (Available from the Program for the Homeless Adults with Serious Mental Illness, Division of Education and Service Systems Liaison, NIMH, 5600 Fishers Lane, Room 11C26, Rockville, MD 20857.)

Samson, C. (1990). Inequality, the New Right and mental health care delivery in the United States in the Reagan Era. *Critical Social Policy Journal, 10*(29), 40-57.

Scheid, T. L., & Wright, E. R. (2017). *A handbook for the study of mental health, 3rd ed,* (pp 266-280). Cambridge: Cambridge University Press.

Schizophrenia. www.nami.org/About-Mental-Illness/Mental-Health-Conditions/Schizophrenia#:~:text=Although%20 schizophrenia%20can%20occur%20at,to%20live%20 well%20with%20schizophrenia

Sharfstein, S. S. (2000). Whatever happened to community mental health? *Psychiatric Services, 5*(5).

Sherin, J., & Stern, H. (2020, Dec 18). Op-Ed: Our mental health laws are failing. www.latimes.com/opinion/story/2020-12-18/ need-for-new-laws-to-address-homelessness

Smith, D. (2019, Nov 6). *These homes kept L.A.'s most vulnerable from being homeless: Now they're clos-ing.* www.latimes.com/california/story/2019-11-06/ homeless-housing-board-care-homes-mental-illness

Sudhakar-Krishnan, V., & Rudolf, M. C. J. (2007). How import-ant is continuity of care? *Archives of Disease in Childhood, 92*(5), 381-383.

Symon, E. (2020, Sept 26). *Several mental health reforing bills signed by Gov. Newsom.* https://californiaglobe.com/

section-2/several-mental-health-reforming-bills-signed-by-gov-newsom/

Tarasoff v Regents of Univ. of Cal. (1976). www.lexisnexis.com/community/casebrief/p/casebrief-Tarasoff-v-regents-of-univ-of-cal

The California Treatment Advocacy Coalition and The Treatment Advocacy Center (2009). *A guide to Laura's Law: California's law for assisted outpatient treatment*. https://www.treatmentadvocacycenter.org/storage/documents/guide-lauras-law-ab1421.pdf

The Mental Health Parity and Addiction Equity Act (nd). https://www.cms.gov/CCIIO/Programs-and-Initiatives/Other-Insurance-Protections/mhpaea_factsheet

Therapy issues for women. (nd). https://www.goodtherapy.org/learn-about-therapy/issues/women-issues

Torrey, E. F. (2014). *American psychosis: How the federal government destroyed the mental illness treatment system.* New York: Oxford University Press.

Treatment Advocacy Center, www.treatmentadvocacycenter.org/about-us

Watson, D. P., Jackson, J., & Adams, E. L. (2017). Mental health policy in the United States: Critical reflection and future directions for sociological research. In T. L. Scheid & E. R. Wright, *A handbook for the study of mental health, 3rd ed*, (pp 573-590). Cambridge: Cambridge University Press.

Wilson, B. B. (2016). Current Gaps in Mental Health Services. Los Angeles County Mental Health Commission, Unpublished report.

Wisner, J. (2021, Nov 5). *No time to waste: An imminent housing crisis for people with serious mental illness living in adult residential facilities.* https://www.chhs.ca.gov/wp-content/uploads/2021/11/Housing-That-Heals-11-05-21.pdf

ABOUT THE AUTHOR

Barbara B Wilson, LCSW, (Licensed Clinical Social Worker) EDPNA
(Eligible for Direct Pay Non-Attorney

Advocacy for mental health services is the driving passion that guides Barbara Wilson's everyday life. She is a Licensed Clinical Social Worker and an Eligible for Direct Pay Non-attorney for Social Security and SSI Claimants.

Ms. Wilson maintained a double major at University of Nebraska, Lincoln and received a bachelor of science degree in 1966, graduating in the top 6% of the university graduates. She achieved her master's degree in social work from the University of Nebraska, Lincoln in 1970. She specialized in psychiatric training in the budding community mental health movement. Her masters thesis: follow-up of a group of students who had been excluded from school pending psychiatric assessments in the Omaha school system. Following graduation, Ms Wilson joined the largest employer of Nebraska, Western Electric Corporation, as a community relations specialist, where she learned corporate methodology and responsibility in community relations. However, Ms. Wilson's first love is working and fighting for the mental health community.

She left the private sector and moved to Denver, Colorado, to gain the necessary skill sets needed from the radical new approach of treating adults with SMI without locked doors. It was an exciting time as public advocacy for greater freedom, control, and humane treatment of the adults with SMI population began to expand. As a practicing mental health professional, she was an early pioneer in public/private partnerships for community activities and creating community-based supportive services.

In 1973 Ms. Wilson relocated to California to work for the State Department of Mental Hygiene where she developed programs, instruction, and support for board-and-care homes in the state. Ms. Wilson's primary focus was to create and monitor community infrastructure for adults, children, and older adults hospitalized in state hospitals. This ensured community safety, mitigated homelessness, and ensured proper stewardship of taxpayer dollars. In 1986, many of those programs were dissolved or disbanded. Ms. Wilson was realigned with the Los

Angeles County Department of Mental Health, where she ultimately retired from the LA County Department of Mental Health in 1992.

Ms. Wilson's return to mental health advocacy was spurred by people in the community who would come to her for help in locating resources for their loved one, often adult children with SMI. In returning to active practice, she learned how decimated community mental health had become. Here are a few results of her activism:

1. She noticed that people going to the Olive View Urgent Care Center via bus were forced to pass the UCC, and continue on to the Olive View main campus 1.5 miles away and then walk back.Located in the San Fernando Valley, summer days can easily top 100 degrees. Extreme exposure to sunlight can be contra-indicated for many people on certain medications. She began by advocating for a bus stop to be installed in front of the UCC. Instead, they installed a Stop Light!

2. In seeking to help families identify licensed Adult Residential Facilities aka Board & Care homes, there was no demarcation on the state Community Care Facilities website. Thus, families spent hours and days calling facilities to learn whether or not the facility accepted referrals with mental disabilities (vs. Intellectual Disabilities). Over a period of time, Ms. Wilson was successful in mobilizing sufficient interest

in this issue to change state policy. AB 1766 was passed and signed by Gov. Newsom in 2020.

3.   In re-connecting with Adult Residential Facilities aka Board & Cares, Ms. Wilson was appalled at the often-run-down condition of the physical plant but with the low-reimbursement rate of $35 per diem there was simply no money in the budget for "extras".

Licensed facilities are required to provide 3 meals daily plus snacks, housekeeping, two-person shared rooms (as opposed to some unlicensed facilities that have 3 sets of bunk beds in a 12 x 14 bedroom); laundry, medications locked, stored, and administered by dose. All for $35 per day. Ms. Wilson decided something had to be done.

To date, she has been able to stimulate interest sufficient to generate a report written by the Mental Health Commission of Los Angeles County. That report stimulated interest from the Los Angeles County Board of Supervisors. The Los Angeles County Board of Supervisors declared it to be a major priority. Eyes are now on Sacramento to find a way to raise the rate of reimbursement to a livable rate competitive with other 24-hour non-medical facilities. In the meantime, Governor Newsom's 2021 budget delivered an earlier promise (pre-Covid) that provides funding for Deferred Maintenance to those ARF's who serve Adults who are Low-Income and who have SMI.

Increased access to quality care and humane treatment of adults with SMI will always be her goal!

Barbara Wilson is the founder and director of Mental Health Hookup, a nonprofit located in the Santa Clarita Valley serving the greater Los Angeles County metropolitan area and Ventura County.

For more information about what YOU can do to advocate for change, contact Barbara B. Wilson LCSW. She will be happy to help you get started.

Proverb: "If everybody does a little, then nobody has to do a lot."

Index